# ANCIENT CRETE : A SOCIAL HISTORY

# STUDIES IN SOCIAL HISTORY

*edited by*

## HAROLD PERKIN

*Senior Lecturer in Social History, University of Lancaster*

◇◇◇◇◇◇◇◇◇◇◇◇◇◇◇◇◇◇◇◇◇◇◇◇◇◇◇◇◇◇◇◇◇◇

# ANCIENT CRETE

## A SOCIAL HISTORY

*From Early Times until
the Roman Occupation*

by

### R. F. Willetts, M.A.

*Reader in Greek in the University of Birmingham*

LONDON: Routledge and Kegan Paul
TORONTO: University of Toronto Press

*First published 1965*
*in Great Britain by*
*Routledge and Kegan Paul Ltd*
*and in Canada by*
*University of Toronto Press*

*Printed in Great Britain*
*by Western Printing Services Ltd, Bristol*

To
My Wife

# Contents

# Plates

The plates are reproduced from photographs by the Author

# Acknowledgements

MY THANKS are due to Dr. W. B. Morgan for drawing
the map of Crete; to Mr. Harold Perkin, M.A., the
Editor of this Series, and to my colleague, Mr.
R. Sawers, M.A., for reading my typescript and
suggesting improvements in presentation; and to
Mrs. Margaret Fisher, Mrs. Barbara Baker and Miss
R. H. Gold for technical assistance.

R.F.W.

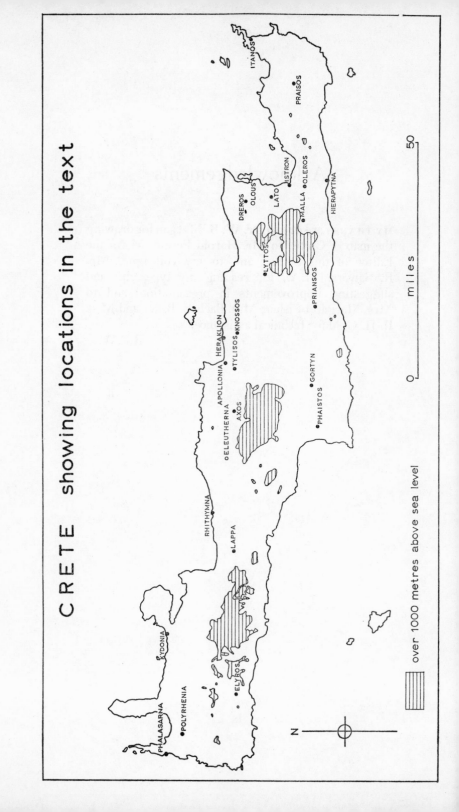

CRETE showing locations in the text

N

0       miles       50

over 1000 metres above sea level

PHALASARNA
POLYRHENIA
KYDONIA
ELYROS
RHITHYMNA
LAPPA
ELEUTHERNA
APOLLONIA
AXOS
HERAKLION
TYLISOS
KNOSSOS
GORTYN
PHAISTOS
DREROS
OLOUS
LYTTOS
LATO
ISTRON
PRIANSOS
MALLA
OLEROS
HIERAPYTNA
ITANOS
PRAISOS

# I

✧✧✧✧✧✧✧✧✧✧✧✧✧✧✧✧✧✧✧✧✧✧✧✧✧✧✧✧✧✧✧✧✧✧✧✧✧

# Introduction

✧✧✧✧✧✧✧✧✧✧✧✧✧✧✧✧✧✧✧✧✧✧✧✧✧✧✧✧✧✧✧✧✧✧✧✧✧

THE interest which has been aroused by the rapid advance of
Cretan studies in recent years is a measure of their importance
for our understanding of the early history of European civilization. It is now generally recognized that the island of Crete
played a part in this early history which is out of all proportion
to its size. Geographically the island forms a bridgehead flank-
ing the southern entrance to the Aegean basin. It performed a
similar role in the historical sense. Roughly equidistant from
Syria and Egypt, it became a centre of maritime trade and was
early influenced by the economic, technical and artistic advances
made by the civilizations of the Ancient Near East. In particular, the use of metal, first copper, then bronze, already long
developed in the East, spread westwards to the coasts of Asia
Minor. During the course of the third millennium B.C., the
Cretans adapted the knowledge they received as a result of their
intercourse with the East and laid the foundations for further
rapid advances. Our own appreciation of the achievements of
Cretan civilization has resulted from the application of three
interrelated classes of evidence—archaeology, linguistics and
the text of Homer.

A hundred years ago there were no accepted objective
criteria, in the form of buildings, pottery, jewellery and armour,
which were relied upon to form an independent witness of the

1

realities of the world which emerges in the Homeric poems. The history of Greece began approximately with the First Olympiad in 776 B.C. Everything that went before, including the Homeric Age, was legend or myth.

Now, what is sometimes described as the Aegean Civilization has been discovered by archaeology. The objective criteria of Greek prehistory reach back to the beginning of the Iron Age, throughout the whole of the Bronze Age, and into Neolithic times.

This thoroughgoing change in outlook has been brought about by the labours of the archaeologists and scholars of many nations. But it chiefly stems from the work of two men in particular, Heinrich Schliemann and Sir Arthur Evans. Schliemann rightly declared that he had discovered a new world for archaeology. His excavations at Troy, Mycenae and Tiryns laid the basis for the later work of others, such as Blegen and Wace, and proved that there was a historical reality behind Homer.

Sir Arthur Evans began to excavate the Bronze Age Palace of Minos at Knossos in Crete over sixty years ago. The main excavations at the Palace were completed during six seasons, from 1900 to 1905. In the process it can be said that Evans virtually discovered the Bronze Age or Minoan civilization of Crete. Other monuments of this civilization were rapidly revealed; and indeed fresh additions to our knowledge are constantly being made. The contents of palaces, villas, houses, settlements, cemeteries and tombs bear witness to Cretan Bronze Age achievements.

This achievement can be measured in all the important areas of central and eastern Crete. The Minoan seafarers went in search of raw materials for their industries from neighbouring countries—gold, silver, tin, lead, copper, ivory, lapis lazuli. They made safe harbours for their merchant ships on small islands and peninsulas. Among these peaceful and energetic people, craftsmen of all kinds enjoyed special favour. Within the limits of their techniques the Minoans set themselves to improve the natural advantages of their island home. They succeeded to a remarkable degree. The ruins of the great palaces show them to have been Europe's first constructional engineers. A network of paved roads, aqueducts, viaducts, irrigation channels, drainage systems, harbour installations, confirm the claim. They excelled in many arts, in addition to the magnificent fresco-painting which has become most commonly associated with them. For they were equally highly skilled in the moulding and hammering of bronze work; in the production of alloyed metals of great strength; in the use of filigree and granulation and soldering as they made their gold objects; in the use of gold and other precious materials for inlaid work, such as silver, ivory and lapis lazuli; in carving stone, even rock crystal, basalt and obsidian. Their pottery was both beautiful and varied, the use of colour in its manufacture unsurpassed. They worked coloured glass into jewels, were the first to make gold and ivory statues, as they were also the first to develop the technique of polychrome faience. Their masterpieces are numerous and most of them are miniatures. But these minatures were often influenced by their paintings.

Of this most immediately arresting of all their arts, Dr. N. Platon has rightly observed: 'Motion is its ruling characteristic; the figures move with lovely grace, the decorative designs whirl and turn, and even the architectural composition is allied to the incessant movement becoming multiform and complex. The art is ruled by conventions, and yet it looks equally naturalistic. The secret life of nature is outspread in man's creation, which imbues it with a special charm and grace. A hymn to Nature as Goddess seems to be heard from everywhere, a hymn of joy and life. The agony of death, so familiar in prehistoric civilization, is not perceptible here.'[1]

The development and brilliant climax of this Minoan era occupied a period of some 1,500 years. Then, towards 1400 B.C., Minoan Crete was afflicted by widespread calamity. Knossos and other cities were violently destroyed, either by enemy assault or by natural disaster, such as earthquakes. Though many of the abandoned sites of towns and villages were reoccupied, the Minoan culture never recovered its supreme vitality. About a hundred years before this disaster it is probable that Mycenaean Greeks from the mainland had penetrated into Crete. One possibility is then that these invaders from Greece, who had previously come under Minoan cultural influence, were responsible for the destruction of the main centres of Minoan civilization.

[1] GAMH 28-9.

The causes of the collapse of the Minoan supremacy in the Aegean have to remain, at least for the time being, conjectural. But it is certain that the centre of power and prestige in the Later Bronze Age shifted to Mycenae on the mainland. Later Greek legends about the greatness of Crete fall into the period of the greatest extension of Minoan influence, from about 1500 to 1400 B.C. The archaeological record, traditional material and actual documents from other lands confirm the spread of Mycenaean influence eastwards between 1400 and 1350 B.C., to Rhodes, Cyprus, Syria and Egypt.

The Mycenaean influence was, however, short-lived. Its collapse, after about two and a half centuries, was but a part of the general collapse of the Bronze Age cultures of the Aegean area. There was a transitional period in Crete, characterized by the appearance of iron and a developing identity with the common pattern of Aegean culture. Mycenaean hegemony had been undermined by new invaders of the mainland. These were the Dorians, a tribal people using Iron Age techniques. From the mainland they went overseas to various areas, including Crete. By the eighth century B.C. all the indications are that they had gained a general supremacy over the island and its cities and villages.

From about this time a new epoch of Cretan history begins. It lasts, in all its essentials, until the Roman conquest of the island in the first century B.C. It is an epoch marked by the establishment of a new social order with quite specific features. The description of these features is the theme of this book.

In the early part of this new epoch, Crete was influenced artistically from the east. During the seventh and sixth centuries B.C., there was indeed something like a renaissance of Cretan art, especially in stone sculpture, clay-plastic and metalwork, stimulated by Oriental influences.

In the Classical period of the fifth and fourth centuries, Crete seemed to play no part in the major achievements of Hellenic civilization. The island is commonly described as a backwater during this time, firmly cast into the mould of the second of those four phases of development typical of ancient Greek society in general—that is to say, monarchy, aristocracy, tyranny and democracy.

For the Greek city-states were typical social organizations of the Iron Age. Compared with the techniques of the Bronze Age, usually the monopoly of minority corporations of ruling classes, the techniques of the Iron Age were much more widely shared, because iron became more plentiful and cheaper and more efficient than bronze. Therefore industry and commerce could make fresh advances. As a result there developed a more extensive division of labour, in agriculture, in handicraft industry and in trade. There were many more varied occupation groups, sharing common interests. As these divisions of labour increased, between the towns and the countryside, between different types of town labour, so there developed new forms of official administration. The old tribal or semi-tribal forms of social organization were replaced by state institutions. The village settlements of former times had been divided by lot into equal shares for all according to their needs. The city-states were, in the beginning, towns governed by a landed nobility, surrounded by satellite villages, inhabited by peasants.

The landed aristocracy, once established within the framework of the new city-states, became more and more privileged, economically and socially. In course of time there grew up, in addition to the peasantry, a whole class of landless people. These landless persons began to settle overseas. That is how the Greeks became dispersed over the Mediterranean area. By the sixth century B.C. they had moved beyond the confines of Greece itself and of the coasts of the Aegean. There were colonies of Greeks on the shores of Thrace and the Black Sea, in Italy and in Sicily, in Spain and Gaul. Consequently there was further expansion of trade. Barter would no longer suffice as a normal means of exchanging goods. Commodity production developed. The invention of coined money followed. Soon all kinds of goods could be bought and sold and mortgaged. Peasant families could be driven off the land, forced into exile, beggary, labour in the mines.

The merchants, the manufacturers, the men in control of money, rapidly increased their wealth. Traditional, landed wealth began to be superseded as the main source of social power and prestige. As moneyed wealth grew, so the old landed aristocracy intensified its exploitation of the peasantry. At the same time the new men of money clamoured for political rights, the peasantry for land.

The social struggles which ensued led to revolutionary up-
heavals in many of the city-states, which, in their turn, culminated in the growth of democratic forms of government.
These social conflicts between the old landed nobility on the
one hand, and, on the other hand, a 'middle' class and a peasantry who were both insisting on changes, issued in the tyranny.
The tyrant, who represented the interests of the new social
groups, expropriated the landed aristocracy and centralized the
administration. The economy of the city-state could be organized
afresh in favour of the classes whose support had made the
tyranny possible. Land reform ensured that peasants were
settled on the land in small holdings. Trade was stimulated,
large schemes of public works, and of urban reconstruction, were
put in hand. There were increasing avenues of employment for
the artisans, as manufacturing developed and as the shibboleths
of the old traditional economy, sponsored by the landed nobility,
were removed.

However, as time went on, the bonds of mutual interest
between the tyrant and the new men who had brought him to
power were often broken. A point was reached when the new
moneyed classes were strongly enough entrenched to dispense
with the tyranny which had fostered their growth. Where this
happened, the tyranny could be replaced by a form of political
organization more directly in keeping with the needs of large-
and small-scale owners of property within the confines of a
money economy. The next stage in revolutionary change after
the tyranny was democracy.

To the Greeks we owe the concept and the first models of
democratic government in history. The first impulses originated
in Ionia, on the eastern shores of the Aegean. Thence the fer-
ment spread along the trade routes as far as the Greek colonies
in Italy and Sicily, as well as to the mainland of Greece. Where
democracy took hold, radical changes were brought about in the
social, economic and political structure of the city-states. There
were also profound repercussions in the spheres of science, of
medicine, of literature, and drama, and of education. But some
parts of the Greek world were relatively unaffected. Sparta, as
well as Crete, remained a conservative, aristocratic society.

There were hundreds of Greek city-states. We are ill-
informed about most of them, fortunately relatively well-

informed about Athens. We also know enough about Sparta to lend plausibility to the view that Athens and Sparta represented the dominant contrast in types of city-state. But this view is an over-simplification of historical realities.

The more we know about the other city-states, the more we are able to set Athens and Sparta in a truer historical perspective. More important still, when we can enlarge our knowledge about conditions of life in places other than Sparta which never became democracies, the better our appreciation of the Athenian achievement.

For ancient democracy achieved its most spectacular growth and achievement in Athens. The Athenians were, with good reason, proud of this new social system. Democracy in antiquity, however, had its limitations, governed by the historical conditions in which it had come into being. The most significant of these limitations was that it was based upon slave labour. Free citizens could devote at least part of their leisure to political affairs, especially if they lived near or inside the city, in the Assembly, the Council or in some elective magistracy. This leisure of the free classes was gained from the surplus wealth which accrued from the exploitation of slave labour. The slaves were chattels, 'live tools', without civic rights or political rights. Ancient democracy was typified by the contradiction that the freedom of the citizen classes was a consequence of the lack of freedom of the slaves.

Primitive forms of ownership of land had completely disappeared with the earlier development of aristocracy and tyranny. The economic foundation of Athenian political democracy was now small-scale peasant agriculture combined with independent handicrafts. The new form of moneyed wealth, which was so closely associated with the growth of democratic institutions, allowed the majority of the Athenians access to forms of private ownership. It became possible for the citizen labourers to be private owners of their own means of labour—as peasants, owners of the land, as artisans, owners of their tools.

The reforms of Kleisthenes in the last decade of the sixth century followed upon the collapse of the Athenian tyranny. A cardinal feature of the democratic structure based upon these reforms was a new tribal system which replaced the primitive, traditional tribal system which had had deep roots in Athenian

7

history. This primitive tribal system had been perpetuated and adapted by the Athenian aristocrats to suit their own interests. The same thing happened, but in rather different conditions, in both Sparta and Crete. But it was now abolished in Athens. The new tribal system gave political expression to the economic domination of the country by the city. The aristocrats had maintained the powers of the phratry (or sub-division of the tribe) and kept it as a closed corporation, as they also preserved the restrictive rights of the hereditary clan. These time-honoured privileges were broken. Under the new system, at least for some time, the whole citizen body regained the forms of its ancient tribal rights, but in a quite new political framework.

The personal freedom of the individual was closely bound up with rights of private ownership. Because forms of private ownership were developed historically by men, the women of Athens enjoyed no political, social and educational privileges. This was the case even in the early and best period of the democracy.

Athenian society at this period was composed of three classes —citizens, metics (settlers from abroad), and slaves. All the citizens were allowed to take part in the Assembly and to form part of the Council. They also had to supply representatives for various offices of varying degrees of importance, and to do various kinds of public service. It became necessary to introduce payment for these public services. In the same way the state allowed public assistance for invalid workmen as well as for war orphans; while in times of hardship corn was either sold cheaply or distributed free.

The citizen population was composed of four different categories, based upon income. The distinctions between these various grades became less sharply defined as democracy became more extensively applied, making it increasingly possible for the poorer citizens to qualify for the highest offices. Even so, social differences continued to exist and the landed aristocracy continued to exercise a good deal of influence for a long time.

Only citizens had political rights, just as citizens alone possessed the land. The more wealthy citizens invested their money in business and in banking, the poorer worked as artisans. Most of the industrial and commercial work was, however, done by the metics and slaves. The metics, cosmopolitan in origin, went into all the industries and controlled shipping. Since they were foreigners, the metics, though encouraged by the government in other ways, did not exercise political rights.

Not many decades of the fifth century had passed before the system of chattel slavery began to seize upon production. Slaves of various kinds had certainly existed in earlier times. But, so long as the economy remained predominantly agrarian, the uses to which slaves could be put were severely restricted. Hence their numbers had been modest. When the coinage was introduced and a money economy developed, with increased trade and manufacture, there were demands for the employment of slaves in workshops, mines, quarries and transport.

Once it became economically feasible, the slave population of Athens quickly increased. Estimates of population in antiquity always have to be conjectural. Nevertheless there is reason to believe that in 431 B.C. the citizens numbered about 170,000, the slave population about 115,000. A census was taken rather more than a century afterwards, in 313 B.C. At that time there were 84,000 citizens and 400,000 slaves.[2]

Since slaves were private property, there was a tendency for wealth in the form of slaves to become restricted to a minority of the citizen population. Wealthy citizens could own hundreds of slaves, the poorer one or two slaves, perhaps none. The poorer citizens were an increasing majority. With the growth of slave labour, free labour declined in value and prestige. The citizens began to use the rights they had won under the democracy to oblige the state to grant them more for doing their civic duties. The cost was met partly by trade and taxes, partly from another source. In the middle of the fifth century the league of free cities which Athens had led against the Persian invaders some three decades earlier was turned into an empire. Revenues from this empire supplemented other dues and taxes. Exactions and expansion led to armed conflict.

Athens and her allies became involved with Sparta and her allies in the prolonged and exhausting Peloponnesian War, from 431 to 403 B.C. At the end the Athenian empire was no more. The word democracy thereafter increasingly assumed the meaning of republican government, as opposed to monarchy.

[2] See further Gomme, PAFFC; Hammond, 329; Thomson, AO 2.357, AA 348; Jones, 161–80.

It was deprived of its radical associations with the early form of Athenian democracy which had given such immense stimulus to the flowering of Hellenic civilization.

It is not difficult to define by hindsight the limitations of ancient democracy. But before the extent of the novelty of the historical changes which its realization brought about can be properly assessed, those changes have to be viewed against the context in which they occurred.

Other considerations apart, this would be an important enough motive for inquiring into the history of ancient Crete. For when we conduct such an inquiry, with the contrast of Athens in mind, we are bound to be faced with the problem of the causes of historical change in the conditions of Greek antiquity; and the conclusions which we draw will have their part to play in the formulation of more general theories about the nature of historical change.

Nor is this kind of inquiry a novel pursuit. The collapse of Athenian democracy brought disillusion and a reaction among more conservative thinkers against social and historical change. Athenian society, from the sixth to the end of the fifth century B.C. had progressed by a rapid series of revolutions. Only in the last few centuries of our own era has the pace of historical change been so rapid. But the democratic system of Athens had been brought to ruin in the mesh of its unresolved contradictions. Now, in the fourth century B.C., the perspectives of social advance had become uncertain. Uncertainty about the future generated doubt and lack of confidence in the heritage of the past. In retrospect, and in comparison with other parts of the Greek world, the Athenian democracy had failed to achieve stability. What has been admired in more recent times as an achievement bordering on the miraculous, no matter how short-lived, came to seem too adventurous because it had not endured.

Therefore, as we can judge from Plato's *Republic* and *Laws*, and from Aristotle's *Politics*, Sparta came to be admired and Crete idealized. Quite suddenly the Cretan backwater seemed to call for study and explanation.

The most abiding heritage of Minoan Crete for the Classical Greek world was its religion. In all kinds of cult Minoan influence was pervasive and abiding.[3] Where cult practices

[3] The evidence is reviewed in my CCF.

endured, it was natural that myth and legend should also be remembered and traced back to a Cretan origin. Minos and the Minotaur, Daidalos, the daring inventor, Theseus and Ariadne, and Pasiphae, wife of Minos, were familiar names. In particular, the Athenians told how Minos had made war against their ancestors and compelled them to send an annual tribute of seven youths and seven maidens to be devoured in the labyrinth by the Minotaur. The Minotaur, the offspring of Pasiphae's intercourse with a bull, was a monster, half man, half bull. Daidalos had made the labyrinth in which the Minotaur lived, until it was killed by Theseus, with the help of Ariadne, daughter of Minos.

But these were romantic fragments from a distant past. Homer, it was true, gave substance to the memory of the flourishing state of Crete in those far-off days. Until interest was revived the little that Herodotos and Thucydides, the great fifth-century historians, have to say about Crete, valuable though it is, fairly reflects the impact that contemporary Crete was making upon the Greek world in general.

Then there occurs this change of attitude. The philosophers begin to look for general principles about the way in which Cretan political and social life were managed. The political theory of antiquity is thereby enriched, particularly the Aristotelian. By good chance the observations of Plato and Aristotle have survived. But the writings of the historians who gave special attention to Crete in the Hellenistic period have disappeared except for fragmentary survivals. There is some authentic information in the work of the historian Polybios, of the second century B.C., but, by his time, Crete was playing a very minor part in the great conflicts between major powers on which his attention is naturally concentrated. Strabo, the geographer, writing over a century later, reports valuable information, but it is largely concerned with religion. We are aware that the Cretan Thaletas flourished in the seventh century B.C. and was said to have journeyed to Sparta to cure a plague by means of his music and stayed to introduce drastic musical reforms. Similarly, the poet Epimenides came to Athens in the time of Solon; but none of his poems survive.[4]

[4] The ancient literary evidence is collected and discussed in my ASAC 152–65 and compared with the epigraphic evidence *ibid*. 166–91; cf. my CCF 301–16 and *passim*, also Van Effenterre, CMG *passim*.

We may be grateful then that, amid the wreckage of Greek lyric poetry, one poem from Crete, perhaps going as far back as the sixth century B.C., did survive into the traditional lyrical corpus. This is the so-called Song of Hybrias.[5] It gives a fascinating glimpse into an early Crete untroubled by the trends towards tyranny and democracy already developed elsewhere. The words are spoken by a Cretan aristocrat.

'My spear and my sword and that fine shield, which guards my skin, are my great wealth. For I plough with this, I reap with this, I tread the sweet wine from the vine with this, I am called master of the serfs with this. But those who dare not hold the spear and sword and that fine shield, to guard their skin, all fall and kiss my knee, calling me master and great lord.'

Such was the written legacy from Crete and about Crete in the historical period up to the Roman conquest which has come down to us. But from the last two decades of the nineteenth century onward our scanty information has been extensively supplemented by archaeological investigation and by the many inscriptions which have come to light in consequence. These inscriptions have now been collected into four great volumes, edited by Professor Margarita Guarducci.[6] This evidence goes back for about three centuries before any precise literary information begins, to the seventh century B.C. even, in fragments. The inscriptions record details of constitutional practice and events of Cretan history from within, from the standpoint of the governing classes of city after city, each with its own particular set of traditions. The generalized Crete of the outside literary observer can now be broken down into its separate parts of time and place. The limits of our knowledge have increased to impressive dimensions. For it so happens that the literary information about Crete is most thorough when the inscriptional evidence is most deficient, that is, in the fourth century B.C. Inscriptions and literary evidence have thus become mutually supporting in a number of ways.

Of all the Cretan inscriptions discovered, the Gortyn Code far surpasses anything else in its importance. The manner of its discovery merits some description.

Gortyn or Gortyna is briefly mentioned by Homer, once in

---

[5] Ath. 15.695f., cf. Eust. 1574.7; Bowra, GLP 398–403; Willetts, CCF 317–23.

[6] *Inscriptiones Creticae opera et consilio Friderici Halbherr collectae* (Rome, 1935–50).

the *Iliad* and once in the *Odyssey*. According to Strabo, the greatest and most famous of the Cretan cities were Knossos, Gortyn and Kydonia (modern Khania).[7] We also know from the archaeological record that other cities, such as Phaistos and Lyttos, were also developed into important centres in the Archaic period of the seventh and sixth centuries. But it was Gortyn which eventually became the capital of the Province of Crete and Cyrene after the Roman conquest of 67 B.C. The extensive and impressive ruins of the city astride the road, in the southern part of the Messara plain, which now runs from Heraklion to Phaistos, testify to its importance in the Roman period.

It was in 1857 that Thenon found an inscribed stone at Gortyn, which was built into the walls of a mill beside a stream. This stone was purchased by Thenon for the Louvre. The archaic nature of the inscription on this stone and the difficulty of extracting a satisfactory sense from it attracted the interest of scholars. However, it was not until 1878 that Bréal was able to prove that the fragmentary inscription dealt with the adoption of children. In the following year, 1879, Haussoullier copied a similar fragment which he saw in a house near the mill. This second fragment was found to be concerned with the rights of heiresses.

Then, in July 1884, Halbherr, a pupil of Comparetti, paid a visit to the site. He was favoured by good fortune. For the water happened to be drawn off from the mill whilst he was there. A short distance below the mill a channel of the stream ran over a wall. Some letters near the top of this wall were pointed out to Halbherr. He made a trench along the inside of the wall and discovered four inscribed columns. The last column to the left was not completely inscribed at the bottom, indicating that it was the end of the whole inscription in that direction. But the inscription still continued to the right into a field. Halbherr could not obtain permission to dig in this field.

The part of the inscription so far revealed had been cut directly upon the layers of stone in the wall, with an extraordinary precision. The wall itself had been made without cement, indicating an archaic technique. The two fragments previously copied by Thenon and Haussoullier were known to have come from the same stream. Now it also became clear that

---

[7] *Il.* 2.646; *Od.* 3.294; Str. 10.476.

they had been taken from the same wall and had formed the upper layers of the inscription.

Halbherr copied the four columns in two days and then returned to Heraklion. Here he met Ernst Fabricius, who had been travelling in western Crete on behalf of the German Institute at Athens. Halbherr told Fabricius about his discovery. Towards the end of October Fabricius went to the site himself. He was able to persuade the owner of the field to allow him to dig a trench along the wall to the limit of the inscription. As a result eight more columns were found, in an excellent state of preservation.

It transpired that the wall on which the twelve columns of the Gortyn Code had been inscribed was circular. If the circle had been complete, the wall would have had a diameter of nearly a hundred feet. This circular wall had supported the structure of a theatre built perhaps in the first century B.C. But it had previously formed part of a much earlier building, perhaps a law-court. Each column of the Code, cut upon four layers of stone, is about five feet high; and the length of the whole inscription is about thirty feet. Each column, except the last, consists of from 53 to 56 lines, the whole amounting to more than 600 lines.

The inscription has been called 'the Queen of Inscriptions', and with good reason. Not only does it amount to an extensive text. It is most impressively cut upon the stone. For the inscription is clearly written in capital letters of about an inch high. It is well preserved and only in a few places, where the blocks join, is it mutilated or illegible. It is written with an alphabet of only eighteen letters, which include F (digamma). Individual letters are of a precise and up-to-date form, highly developed versions of the old Gortynian alphabet. Breaks between paragraphs are marked by a space, filled with a stylized leaf or flower in red paint. The whole inscription begins on the right and ends on the left and the writing on the columns is in the *boustrophedon* ('as an ox turns in ploughing') style, that is to say, with alternate lines facing in opposite directions. The state of the alphabet, the forms of the letters, analysis of linguistic data and comparison with other types of evidence have led to general acceptance of the dating of the Code to the fifth century B.C., perhaps about 480–460 B.C., though some would prefer to say not earlier than about 450 B.C. But there is little doubt that the Code contains older material, incorporating the sanctions of a customary tradition reaching back several centuries earlier.

The dual copying of the inscription led to a dual publication. Fabricius and Comparetti were responsible for these first versions, the German in 1884 and the Italian in 1885. Other editions, translations and commentaries have followed. Both the language and the subject-matter are very difficult and there are problems in both fields which have not been solved. But the main principles are clear.

The availability of this, the first European law-code, and the most important social document of its time, is an immense gain. With the Gortyn Code as our point of departure and chief source of reference for our knowledge of the social system in one of the most prominent Cretan cities in the first part of the fifth century B.C., we can, with the help of the literature and the other inscriptional material, reconstruct many main features of a Cretan society which invited so much interest in antiquity.

# II

<hr>

# The Coming of the Dorians

<hr>

J ust as the progress of archaeology has immensely enriched our knowledge about Greek prehistory, so the science of historical linguistics has set in a new perspective the unique importance of the Greek language and the literary tradition which it embodies. That is because the Greek language has been continuously cultivated as a means of literary expression from Bronze Age times and also because it has survived with relatively so few changes compared with other European languages. No other European language presents such a long and ample record for evolutionary study.

The various types of early Cretan script which appeared in the course of archaeological investigation were divided by Evans into pictographic and linear scripts. The linear scripts were further divided into Linear A and Linear B. The earliest pictographic signs, of the third millennium B.C., are engraved on seals. It is still doubtful whether they represent actual writing. Pictographs of a more developed kind date from about 2000 B.C., on seals and also on tablets and bars, their signs resembling the Hittite signary and Egyptian hieroglyphs.

The Linear Script A appears about the middle of the seventeenth century B.C. and the Linear B Script in the course of the fifteenth century B.C. Both are pre-alphabetic cursive scripts; but pictorial signs continued to be used until the end of Minoan times.

16

Documents in the script known as Linear B were discovered at Knossos over fifty years ago. About the same time a few examples of the same script were found at Thebes and other places in mainland Greece. But it was not until 1939 that actual tablets like those from Knossos were found in mainland Greece, near Messenian Pylos; and it was not until after the Second World War that they were found at Mycenae itself.

Before the tablets were found at Pylos, European scholars had made attempts to read the script, without much success. But the discovery of what might be the palace accounts of King Nestor of Pylos provided fresh stimulus. By 1951, the late Michael Ventris had made a tentative decipherment. Then, in collaboration with Mr. John Chadwick, an account of his proposed decipherment was published in the *Journal of Hellenic Studies* for 1953.

Mr. Ventris made the following claims: (i) that the language of all Linear B documents is an early form of Greek, pre-Dorian but allied to classical Arcadian and Cyprian; (ii) that the script is in the main a syllabary, akin to the classical Cyprian syllabary (nearly all Cyprian inscriptions are written in a special syllabary); and (iii) that by studying the way in which the syllabic signs are used—their frequency, position in the word, combination of one sign with another, and so on—and by inferring the content of the documents from certain signs which are not syllabic but ideographic, it is possible to discover the phonetic value of most of the syllabic signs. Mr. Ventris described how he carried out the work of decipherment.

Most of the Linear B texts are written on small tablets of clay. The scribes first ruled a series of parallel lines on the moist surface of the clay and then wrote from left to right between the lines and from top to bottom of the tablet. Short groups of signs, evidently words, were divided from each other by a short vertical stroke. Most, or all, of the tablets seem to contain lists of people, animals and commodities of various kinds. The writing consists partly of words, which sometimes occur singly or in short sequences, and sometimes in longer sequences, amounting perhaps to continuous prose. But it also consists of ideograms, representing commodities, quantities, values and numerals. Wherever the Linear B script is found, the signs are virtually the same in number and form, and words, both singly and in groups, recur in one place and another. Hence it seems that there is one language in use in all localities. Conversely, there is no indication of a second language in any locality.

The proposed decipherment of Ventris was accepted by a majority of scholars. But other scholars, including Professor A. J. Beattie of Edinburgh and Professor E. Grumach of Berlin, did not accept the decipherment.

When he published his criticism in the *Journal of Hellenic Studies* for 1956, Professor Beattie made these remarks: '. . . when Mr. Ventris proceeds to argue, on historical and archaeological grounds, that the language of the tablets is Greek, it is impossible to refute him. Many scholars in the past have held this view, and many still hold it. I, too, am ready to admit that the language is as likely to be Greek as anything else, although I maintain that there are other possibilities. The question that concerns me now is whether, given that the tablets may be written in Greek, Mr. Ventris' decipherment is correct.'

Other scholars would argue that, even if the criticisms based on linguistic grounds of Beattie and Grumach had been systematically refuted—as they have not—the poverty of the present documents and the difficulty of their interpretation cannot allow them to be used as yet as historical evidence.

The Linear B tablets found by Evans at Knossos were assigned by him to the Late Minoan II period ending about 1400 B.C. The mainland tablets date to the destruction of Pylos and Mycenae round about 1200 B.C. Yet the writing is essentially the same. This has caused speculation and controversy. It could be, of course, that the form of writing was so traditionally fixed that innovation was not encouraged. But it has also been suggested that the apparent discrepancy in the dating might be overcome by a re-examination of the evidence for the Knossian dating at 1400 B.C. So far the suggested re-dating of the end of Knossos has won little support.[1]

The Greeks of historical times learnt many inventions from their eastern neighbours, the greatest being the art of alphabetic writing. The Minoans before them were similarly indebted, and investigation of the connexions between the various Minoan writing systems and Anatolian and Oriental forms of writing could yield some most interesting results.

[1] Palmer, MM; Palmer-Boardman, KT; Hutchinson, PC 90.

As for alphabetic writing—one of the most decisive achievements in the history of early civilization—it is of course known beyond doubt that the North Semitic script was the model for the Greek. There are examples of the model and the copy in their early stages. There is no surviving example of the Greek alphabet which can be dated earlier than the eighth century B.C. The Cretan alphabet is the closest of all to the Semitic Phoenician and it has long been agreed that Crete, was if not the birthplace, at least one of the earliest receivers of the Greek alphabet.

The Babylonian cuneiform script had been systematized as a syllabary, with each sign forming a particular combination of consonant and vowel. The Egyptian script, however, continued as a mixture of pictograms, ideograms and phonograms, including even a few alphabetic signs. The Phoenicians fashioned the Egyptian signs into an alphabet of twenty-two characters. This alphabet had no vowels because Phoenician also shared that characteristic of marked vowel gradation which belongs to the Semitic group of languages, enabling a reader to supply vowels from the context. Phoenician signs were related to Egyptian in their form and meaning but not in their phonetic value.

Some time in the early part of the first millennium B.C., Ionic-speaking Greeks, now settled on the Aegean coast of Anatolia, adopted the Phoenician alphabet. Some Phoenician signs which denoted consonants not existing in Greek were now used as vowels. In the course of the Greek colonial expansion of the eighth and seventh centuries B.C., the new Greek alphabet manifested itself in a number of local variants. These fall into the two main groups of East and West Greek. The later standard form of the Greek alphabet was derived from the Attic, included in the East Greek group. The Cypriot Greeks were exceptional in that they continued to use a pre-alphabetic script, the Cypriot syllabary, until as late as the third century B.C.

Though the study of the transmission of the Greek alphabet takes us back only to the eighth century B.C., we gain illuminating insight into Greek prehistory from the study of the Greek dialects. This specialized study produced a theory which, with slight variations, was accepted over the past half-century, until recently.[2]

Greek city-states had their characteristic local dialects. These

2 Chadwick, GDGP.

many local dialects were distributed into five main groupings by the Classical period. They were: (1) the *Attic-Ionic*, (2) the *Arcado-Cyprian*, (3) the *Aeolic*, (4) the *Doric*, and (5) the *Northwestern*.

When the Dorians had come into Greece and after the consequent Ionian migrations, these dialect groupings became distributed in the following way: (1) *Attic* was the dialect of Attica and *Ionic* of Euboia, the central Aegean and Ionia; (2) *Arcado-Cyprian*, of Arcadia and Cyprus; (3) *Aeolic*, of Boiotia, Thessaly and Aiolis; (4) *Doric*, of the south and east Peloponnese, the south Aegean and south-west Anatolia; (5) *Northwestern*, of the north-west Peloponnese, the Ionian Islands and central Greece. There were further extensions and modifications during and after the period of colonization.

Now the ancients, from the time of Hesiod, distinguished three groups of Greek-speaking peoples, namely (a) Ionians, (b) Dorians, and (c) Aeolians. Modern scholars accepted these categories as a rough basis of classification, for the *Ionic* and *Doric* dialects were plainly recognizable.

*Ionic* was divided into (a) *Attic* and (b) *Ionic*. *Doric* was divided into (a) *North-west Greek* and (b) the *Doric* proper of the Peloponnese and the southern Aegean islands, including Crete. *Lesbian*, *Thessalian* and *Boiotian* were grouped together as *Aeolic*. But another group, *Arcado-Cyprian*, had to be designated to explain the common elements of the dialects of Arcadia and Cyprus. This further group was closely linked with *Aeolic*.

On this basis, a scheme of genetic relationships between the dialects was proposed, though it was not entirely satisfactory; and the whole general theory was associated with the premise of three or more waves of Greek infiltration of the mainland.

Of these waves of infiltration, *Doric* was the most recent. It could obviously be linked with the 'Dorian invasion' or what the ancients themselves described as 'The Return of the Herakleidai'. It was more difficult to postulate pre-Dorian migrations, but most scholars favoured the idea of two separate infiltrations —*Ionian* and *Achaean* or *Aeolian*. The names were used indiscriminately on the view that *Arcado-Cyprian* was nothing more than the southern branch of *Aeolic*.

It was clear that the dialects of Arcadia and Cyprus must go back to a widespread *Achaean* dialect (i.e. the Greek of the period of Achaean or Mycenaean supremacy of the later Bronze Age), which elsewhere was overlaid or replaced by the Dorian immigration. The colonization of Cyprus, from the archaeological evidence, must have begun in the Mycenaean period. Hence it could be inferred that this *Achaean* substratum was the common dialect of southern Greece at that time. But legend told of Ionians in the northern parts of the Peloponnese and it was thought that there must have been either (*a*) an Ionian invasion followed by an Achaean or (*b*) an Achaean invasion followed by an Ionian. However, the evidence for the replacement of Ionians by Achaeans is scanty and insecure. When Herodotos[3] says that at one time the Ionians occupied the part of the Peloponnese subsequently called Achaea, this does not prove that they were expelled by Achaeans. It could mean no more than that Attica and Achaea once formed parts of a linguistic unity. Also, when Pausanias[4] says that, before the return of the Herakleidai, the Argives spoke the same dialect as the Athenians, this does not prove that Argos spoke Ionic.

In the archaeological record there is a clear break between Early and Middle Helladic (*c.* 1900 B.C.). This break is now generally equated with the arrival of the first infiltration of Greek-speaking immigrants. There is another but much less decisive break between Middle and Late Helladic—in fact, the Mycenaean period—round about 1600 B.C. All this has been used to support a theory of two pre-Dorian immigrations.

From the purely linguistic point of view there are some major difficulties in determining the place of *Ionic*. A separation into (*a*) *Attic* and (*b*) *Ionic* can be referred back to migrations in prehistory. But then arises the question: what were its earlier affinities? In trying to meet this problem, Professor George Thomson had argued, in 1949, that there had never been any Ionians in the Peloponnese. That was simply the name given in later times by the Ionians of Ionia to their Achaean ancestors; and further, that *Ionic* was from the beginning a mixed dialect, formed by the fusion of *Achaean* (already subjected to *proto-Ionic* influence) with a variety of local vernaculars, including *Attic*. Dialectal studies by Porzig and Risch in 1954 and 1955 also led to the conclusion that an Ionic invasion of Greece was a fiction. For it now appears that various innovations in which *Ionic*

[3] 7.94.    [4] 2.37.3.

agrees with *Doric* were introduced at the time of the Dorian migrations; and therefore that, at the close of the second millennium, a dialect of the *Arcadian* type was for a time under the influence of *Doric*. This influence soon ceased, and the dialect then proceeded on its independent course of development, only subsequently dividing into the two branches of (*a*) Attic and (*b*) Ionic.[5]

*Doric* was introduced by the Dorians, *North-western* by the Thessaloi and Aitoloi, towards the end of the second millennium B.C. As Thomson has subsequently pointed out, from what Herodotus tells us of the Ionian migration it may be inferred that the *Ionic* dialect assumed the form in which we know it only after that event. Furthermore, since *North-western* elements are found in *West Aeolic* (the *Aeolic* of Boiotia and Thessaly) but not in *East Aeolic* (that of Aiolis), it may be inferred that the Aeolic migration took place before the intrusion of *North-western*. Since *Arcado-Cyprian* elements have been traced in the *Doric* of all parts, it may also be inferred that *Doric* was superimposed on *Arcado-Cyprian*; and also, because of the close affinity between *Arcado-Cyprian* and *Aeolic*, that these two dialects were descended from the Greek of the Achaeans of the Mycenaean period. Finally, because *Arcado-Cyprian* has certain characteristics in common with *Attic-Ionic*, it may be that in the north-east of the Peloponnese, and perhaps elsewhere, it had been superimposed on an older dialect from which was descended the later *Attic-Ionic*.[6]

The position of *Aeolic* is still not clearly determined and it could still be the case that the name represents a separate infiltration of Greek-speakers. However that may be, it is possible to suppose, round about 1200 B.C., a dialectal distribution on the following lines. The Dorians were in the extreme north-west, perhaps in contact with (non-Greek) Illyrians; the Mycenaeans were occupying the whole of southern Greece, perhaps extending as far north as Boiotia; the Aeolians would be forming a kind of buffer between the two, so cutting off the Dorians from the Aegean.[7]

---

[5] Thomson, SAGS I², 390–2, 515–26; W. Porzig *Sprachgeographische Untersuchungen zu den altgriechischen Dialekten* in *Indogermanische Forschungen* 61 (1954) 147–69; E. Risch *Die Gliederung der griechischen Dialekte in neuer Sicht* in *Museum Helveticum* 12 (1955) 61–76.

[6] Hdt. 1.146; Thomson, GL 32.        [7] Chadwick, GDGP 48.

The position in Crete at that time cannot be exactly determined. But we do gain some invaluable information from a famous passage of the *Oydssey*. The relevance of this evidence cannot be discussed, however, without some prefatory remarks about Homer and the Homeric question, in the light of the archaeological and linguistic background just outlined.

The Homeric question is not a problem conjured up by modern scholars. Their great Hellenistic predecessors disputed whether the epics had been composed by the same man. Nowadays, a simple unitarianism is on the retreat and what is fashionably called an analyst view, based on the comparative study of epic style in other languages than Greek—including recent epic composition—is becoming more generally accepted.

One of the scholars who gave impetus to this view was the late Milman Parry. The importance of Parry's work—he died a premature death in 1935—was for some time overlooked except by a few other scholars. Not only did Parry appreciate the significance of the modern oral poetry of Yugoslavia; he showed that the Homeric poems had been oral compositions, which had been built upon a gradually evolved, traditional stock of fixed, formulaic phrases covering many common ideas and contexts. His work is now widely recognized, though not many of those who now rightly praise his work seem to be aware of its relationship to the work of Radlov at the end of the last century or to that of H. M. Chadwick in the earlier part of this century.

'For Homer,' wrote Parry, 'as for all minstrels, to versify was to remember—to remember words, expressions, phrases from the recitals of minstrels who had bequeathed to him the traditional style of heroic verse.'[8] In other words, the Homeric poems were transmitted over many centuries by means of oral tradition through the performances of professional minstrels, performances which were at once improvisations and re-creations, maintaining the stock phrases and epic formulae, adding new material as they went on being recited in the Iron Age, though in the main evoking a pre-Dorian world of the Bronze Age—until they were finally committed to writing, according to tradition, in Athens, at the end of the sixth century B.C.

Homeric archaeology is a comparative study, whose purpose

[8] FMH 6.

is to examine and interpret archaeological data against the background of the poems. Certain features of the poems, such as the descriptions of material objects and social usages, have been dated by archaeologists to specific periods, from the fifteenth century to the seventh. The site of Troy has been identified with Hissarlik, an ancient settlement near the coast of the Aegean in the north-west corner of Asia Minor. Here the remains show evidence of repeated demolition, destruction and rebuilding. The Homeric city is now considered to be Troy VIIa.[9] The city sacked by the Achaeans under Agamemnon belonged to the same culture as their own Mycenae.

The language of the Homeric poems is different from other Greek dialects. It is a mixture, chiefly of *Aeolic* and *Ionic*, with much *Arcado-Cyprian* and some *Attic*. The conclusions derived from study of Homeric linguistics are not, generally speaking, at variance with Homeric archaeology. The source of the epic tradition is the Mycenaean Age. When the arrival of the Dorians compelled other Greek speakers from the mainland to emigrate, this epic tradition was carried over into Asia. Then it was developed and refined, perhaps not far from Smyrna and Chios, by generations of bards who were descended from former inhabitants of Thessaly and Boiotia or from the Peloponnese.[10]

Fortified by more than a half-century of archaeological discovery, accompanied by intense linguistic analysis, the modern reader of Homer can attend to his text, not merely with pleasure, but with something of the same respect for authority that exalted the reputation of the poet in Greek antiquity. But it is a different kind of authority, the authority, not sharply defined, and often indeed obscure, of an actual historical background, with roots in the late Bronze Age and sometimes harking back to the collapsed Minoan civilization once centred in Crete.

Homer has much to say about Crete. For present purposes comment may be concentrated upon a single passage from the nineteenth book of the *Odyssey*, among the most important of all Homeric references to Crete. An Odyssean traveller's tale with a Cretan background is a recurrent theme of the second half of the

[9] The accepted view of the date of the fall of Troy and the identification of Homeric Troy has recently been challenged, however, by Carl Nylander in *Ant.* 37.145.6–11. But see Mylonas PTDF.

[10] Thomson, SAGS I², 435–577; cf. Davison in Wace-Stubbings 234–65; Kirk 271–300.

*Odyssey.* Details change, but the underlying substance is the same. Disguised Odysseus pretends to be a prominent Cretan chieftain who is in some relationship with, and also subordinate to, Idomeneus. Idomeneus is an Achaean with a conventional short pedigree of three generations before the Trojan War.

Piracy and raiding seem to be normal means of supplementing wealth provided by landed estates. Unsettled conditions prevail in Crete. Dissension is provoked by personal rivalry and vendetta. Similar conditions apply overseas. A freebooter may make his fortune, or, with a different sort of luck, he may be kidnapped and sold into slavery. The principal character of the Homeric story has himself done a lot of raiding before the Trojan War. He is portrayed as just the kind of adventurer who was perhaps not at all uncommon in the age of the Aegean sea-raiders who harassed Egypt and other places roughly at about the time of The Trojan War.

The story is presented more lengthily when Penelope wants the still disguised Odysseus to explain about his circumstances in more detail. As a preface to his story, he says:[11]

'Out in the midst of the wine-dark sea, there is a land called Crete, fair and fertile, sea-girt. Therein are many men, countless men, and ninety cities. They have a mixture of languages. For there are Achaeans, stout-hearted Eteocretans, Kydonians, Dorians with their three tribes, god-like Pelasgians. There too is Knossos, a mighty city, where Minos used to be king for nine years, a familiar of mighty Zeus.'

To what extent can these tantalizing details of Cretan ethnography be plausibly assigned to the period round about 1200 B.C., in the same way as we have suggested that the social conditions inherent in the fiction of the Cretan adventurer may be assigned to the same period?

Evans took the view that the name of Idomeneus, the Achaean leader of the Cretan contingent in the army of Agamemnon before Troy, seems to point to early settlement in the land round Ida. Further, that the Achaean dominion over central Crete as suggested in the Catalogue of Ships in the 2nd book of the *Iliad* (which need not exclude the participation of other

---

[11] *Od.* 19.172–9.

Hellenic elements such as the Dorian), seems to offer a real glimpse of historic conditions in Crete at the beginning of the Iron Age. On the other hand, argued Evans, the attempt to annex Minos and to thrust back Achaean or Dorian dominion in Crete into the glorious days of Minoan history was but part of a process of which other traces are perceptible. One such trace he found (following Beloch) to be supplied by an interpolation in the passage of the *Odyssey* under discussion. 'The interpolator', he wrote, '—regardless of the order of composition or even of the most obvious grammatical requirements—has broken into the sentence "Ninety cities and among them Knossos" to insert a brief summary of the later ethnography of the island—including an allusion to the three Dorian tribes.'[12]

The late Miss H. L. Lorimer, writing some thirty years later, found the Crete mirrored in the *Iliad* Catalogue's selection from her hundred towns to be the Crete of the Achaean occupation in Late Helladic III, the later Bronze Age.[13] The situation of these seven towns of Central Crete is the region containing the road that links the ports of her northern and southern coasts. That it was occupied by the Achaeans is plain from the lines in the *Odyssey*[14] which mention Achaeans, Eteocretans and Kydonians and give the main division into centre, east and west. 'They are not necessarily interpolated as 177 certainly is, but even if they are, their evidence is none the worse for that.' (Line 177 has the reference to Dorians and Pelasgians.)

Evans referred to the interpolation 'recently exposed by Professor Beloch, but which, when once attention has been called to it, must command general recognition'. In fact, owing to the increase in our knowledge over the past three decades, Beloch's supposed exposure now must command much less general recognition. It might therefore be safer to withold even a partial recognition and accept the passage as genuine despite the consequent difficulties, until we know more than we do know at present concerning the early Dorian occupation both of Crete and of the mainland. Nevertheless it must be frankly acknowledged that it is the mention of the Dorians in the passage that is its most puzzling feature.

The least difficulty is now caused by the allusion to the

---

[12] Evans, PM 1.10–12; Beloch, *Origini Cretesi. Ausonia* 4 (1910), 220–1.
[13] Lorimer, 47.    [14] *Od.* 19.175–6.

Achaeans, in keeping with the tradition derived from the *Iliad* of their dominion over central Crete. Now when Strabo, the geographer, commented upon the passage of the *Odyssey* which we have been discussing, he quoted the historian Staphylos of Naukratis as saying that the Dorians occupied the part of Crete towards the east, the Kydonians the western part, the Eteocretans the southern, and to these latter belonged the town of Praisos, where there was the temple of Diktaian Zeus; whereas the other peoples, since they were more powerful, dwelt in the plains. It is reasonable, he continued, to suppose that the Eteocretans and the Kydonians were autochthonous, i.e. indigenous, peoples and that the others, i.e. the Dorians, were foreigners, who, according to Andron (the fourth-century B.C. writer on genealogical relationships between Greek tribes and cities) came from Thessaly, from the country which in earlier times was called Doris.[15] The most interesting feature of this comment, so far as the Dorians are concerned, is the information that there was a Doric community or, more likely, communities, presumably small, in the extreme east of the island, beyond Praisos.

A further inference from Strabo's comment is that the Eteocretans represented a now reduced element of the earlier pre-Greek inhabitants of Crete. Praisos, which he mentions as belonging to them, lay in the centre of the eastern tip of the island. The people of Praisos apparently preserved their ancient, distinct language at least until the third century B.C. For a number of inscriptions are extant on which the 'Eteocretan' language is recorded—but it is written in the Greek alphabet. We might gather some very interesting information if these inscriptions can be properly deciphered. We might, for example, gain some clearer conception of the non-Greek language, or languages, once spoken in Greece, Crete, the other islands, and (no doubt in rather a different form) in the south-west of Asia Minor.

Moreover, from what Herodotos[16] has to say about the Praisians, it is apparent that they must have had close connexions with the old Minoan stock. It is then reasonable to conclude that the Praisians could exemplify a most interesting continuation, well into historical times, of those Cretan links

[15] Str. 10.475.         [16] 7.170.

with Asia Minor which typify the institutions of the island in the Bronze Age.

Kydonia (the modern Khania) lay on the north-west coast of Crete, facing the mainland Peloponnese. Herodotus[17] tells how the city was founded in 524 B.C. by Samians, who after flourishing there for a brief period of five years, were reduced to slavery. The earlier importance of the Kydonians is, however, clear from the evidence of Strabo and it is confirmed by Homer.

Strabo[18] explains that the greatest and most famous of the Cretan cities were Knossos, Gortyn and Kydonia. Minos gained the mastery of the sea, divided the island into three parts and founded a city in each part, with both Kydonia and Knossos lying to the north.

The fact is certainly that Knossos continued to be important from Minoan times throughout the historical period. Phaistos became less important after the Minoan age and occupied a subordinate position to that of Gortyn in historical times. Minoan remains at Kydonia go at least as far back as the middle of the second millennium B.C.; and many Minoan remains have been found in caves and elsewhere on the neighbouring peninsula of Akrotiri, north-east of Khania. Hence it has been inferred that the whole of this peninsula was densely populated by the end of the Bronze Age, if not earlier. The evidence of Homer confirms that the Kydonians played a part of some importance in the west at the time.

Nestor describes in the *Odyssey*[19] how it was that Menelaos was absent when Agamemnon was murdered after the return from Troy. He and Menelaos were sailing together from Troy and got as far as Sounion, the southern headland of Attica. Here Menelaos was obliged to stay for a time, while Nestor went on his way. Then Menelaos too set sail with his ships. They ran into a gale off Cape Malia, the south-eastern promontory of Laconia. The gale was severe enough to compel him to divide his ships. Menelaos, with five ships, was driven on by the weather to Egypt. The other part of his contingent made for Crete, or that part of it 'where the Kydonians lived, round about the waters of the Iardanos. At the border of Gortyn, in the murky sea, there is a smooth rock that runs sheer into the water, where the south wind thrusts the mighty swell upon the headland

<hr />

[17] 3.59.          [18] 10.476.          [19] 3.276–300.

on the left, towards Phaistos, and a tiny stone wards off the swell.' Here the ships were wrecked, though the crews escaped.

Some details of this exact description have long been in dispute. But it seems likely that the ships were lost outside the port of Komo. This was the terminus of the great road which ran to the south from Knossos, the centre through which trade passed to and from Egypt in the Bronze Age. The description indicates that the port lay in the territory of the Kydonians, yet was also near the fringe of Gortyn's territory. Gortyn's neighbour to the east, Phaistos, is mentioned; but it seems clear that Gortyn was then, in Mycenaean times, rather more extensive and prominent than it had been in the earlier Minoan period.

Now the Kydonia of later historical times was situated on the north-west coast. Yet, in the Homeric description, the ships were sailing along the south coast when the wreck occurred. Assuming the authenticity of the description, we have to suppose that the Kydonians were at that time spread over the whole extent of the western part of the island. Their territory would have included the south coast as far as the cape where Komo lay, and which also happened to be the border fringe of Gortyn. They lived, according to the Homeric description, round about the 'streams of the Iardanos'. This name is presumably Semitic, the equivalent of 'Jordan'. If so, the non-Greek origin of the Kydonians, implicit in Strabo's account, is to some extent confirmed.

Homer and Strabo, however, distinguish Kydonians from Eteocretans. It may be that the Kydonians who were living in western Crete in Achaean times were of different stock from the Eteocretans, and were perhaps (though for Strabo autochthonous like the Eteocretans), in fact later Bronze Age arrivals from Asia Minor.

Larisa was a characteristic place-name of the Pelasgians. Since it occurs in Crete, we have independent evidence of their presence in the island. For example, Cretan Larisa was, according to Strabo, absorbed by Hierapytna; and there was a tradition that Gortyn had once been called Larisa. The name is found, apart from Crete, in various parts of Thessaly, Attica, Argolis, Elis, the Troad, Aiolis and Lydia. Bearing in mind some survivals in his own day, Herodotus inferred that the Pelasgian language was not Greek. The Pelasgians appear to have been closely related to both Lydians and Etruscans; and the languages of all three peoples, it is thought, were also related. Now the main area of Pelasgian habitation was the North Aegean, in particular the Macedonian coast and the islands of Samothraike, Lemnos and Imbros. We can trace them through the Hellespont and Propontis along the north coast of Anatolia. Hence they may have ultimately derived from the far side of the Black Sea; and it is possible that they did not arrive in Crete before the beginning of the second millennium B.C.[20]

It seems then reasonable to believe that the population of Crete could have included, by the beginning of the twelfth century, Achaeans, Eteocretans, Kydonians and Pelasgians. Therefore it may be wise not to exclude the Dorians at this stage but to hope for confirmation of their presence so early. Nevertheless, since Homer's picture is of a pre-Dorian Greece, to acknowledge the early presence of Dorians alongside the Achaeans only in Crete does face us with a complicated problem. We can make Homer thoroughly consistent if, arguing a later interpolation, we exclude the Dorians from Crete at the time. But our confidence in this kind of solution is bound to be shaken, after we have compared the remarks of Evans and Miss Lorimer on the crucial passage of the *Odyssey* which we have been considering.

Can we, in fact, reasonably entertain the possibility that a group of Dorians had followed the Achaeans into Crete perhaps more than a century before they arrived in strength elsewhere? It is agreed that the Dorians usually possessed themselves only of mainland areas and islands already inhabited by Greek-speakers; compared with earlier arrivals, they did not take over places occupied by older indigenous populations.[21] This general consideration apart, we can find some ancient authority for the tradition of early Dorian habitation in Crete.

We learn from Diodorus that Tektamos, the son of Doros, came from Thessaly, with Aeolians and Pelasgians, and founded a new régime in Crete. Tektamos has been placed in the generation of 1330 B.C. When Strabo states his view that the Eteocretans and Kydonians were autochthonous, he also repeats an opinion that the Dorians were foreigners who came from

[20] Str. 9.440; St. Byz. s.v. Γόρτυν; H. *Il.* 2.841, Str. 9.430, 440, 13.620–1, Paus. 2.24.1, 7.17.5; Hdt. 1.57, 94, Th. 4.109, Str. 5.221, A. *Supp.* 246–7, *Pr.* 860, Hecat. *fr.* 334; Willetts, CCF 135–6.   [21] Nilsson, HM 239.

Thessaly, from the country which in earlier times was called Doris.[22]

The ethnographic passage of the 19th book of the *Odyssey* then has a special significance for establishing a partial, even though in some ways a puzzling, picture of Crete in the age of transition from the Bronze Age to the Iron Age after the Trojan War. This record at least confirms Herodotos in suggesting a time of confusion and trouble, of an intermingling of peoples, following upon which the Greek-speakers who had formed the minority in Mycenaean times became the dominating element as Doric Greek spread over the whole island.

According to the tradition reported by Herodotos, Minos went to Sicily in seach of Daidalos, where he perished by violent death. After a while the Cretans, all except the Polikhnites and the Praisians, launched a great expedition into Sicily. They besieged Kamikos for five years, then called off the siege and went home. They had reached Iapygia on their return voyage when a furious storm broke their ships in pieces. Unable to return to Crete, they founded the town of Hyria and changed their name to Messapian Iapygians. Crete was now stripped of its inhabitants and, according to Praisian (i.e. Eteocretan) tradition, people of various nations flocked there, Greeks above all. The Trojan War occurred three generations after Minos died and the Cretans were not the least distinguished of those who helped Menelaos. However, when they came back from Troy, famine and pestilence attacked both men and cattle. Once again Crete was stripped of its inhabitants, but for a remnant who formed, along with fresh settlers, the third of the Cretan peoples by whom the island had been inhabited.[23]

This third population was presumably the Dorian. Herodotos also hints at some kind of conflict between Cretan and Achaean interests. This may well have been the case, and there may also have been a drastic reduction of the older Minoan population in consequence of various overseas expeditions.

However, the date of the arrival of Dorians with their own dialect of Greek is but one of several major problems whose focus is the island of Crete in the Bronze Age. Homer thought of Crete, as we have seen, as an island of ninety cities, with intermingled tongues. Five peoples are named: the Eteocretans,

[22] D.S. 4.60.2; Str. 10.475, cf. Hdt. 1.56; Myres, WWG 346.    [23] 7.170–1.

Kydonians, Pelasgians, Achaeans and Dorians. Even if Dorians are cautiously dismissed from the Homeric text as a post-Mycenaean addition, the rest of the account probably does date from heroic times, the later Later Bronze. If Achaean be Greek and Etocretan both the language of the Praisians and of the Minoan civilization, the other two languages, Kydonian and Pelasgian, are not likely to have been the same as, or even closely related to, either of them. Hence the classical philologist with an interest in early Crete and Aegean prehistory is not likely to lack stimulus for his researches in the next decade or so, as each new tentative answer perhaps multiplies his problems.

Fresh evidence must be forthcoming before we can present a satisfactory account of the Dorian invasion in general at the end of the Bronze Age. The difficulties inherent in the whole problem, so far as the mainland is concerned, lie beyond the scope of this book. However, some points of comment must be made. Although some modern scholars have expressed scepticism about the reality of a 'Dorian invasion', Greek tradition about it was so strong and modern evidence so far accumulated so convincing that the majority of scholars agree that, if there were no tradition of an invasion, we should have to suppose that it did occur. Yet *Dorian* or *Doric* is more valid as a linguistic than a racial term. What is called a 'Dorian invasion' was associated, in Greek tradition, with the Return of the Herakleidai, the 'Sons of Herakles', who may have been an Achaean tribal grouping, tracing its descent from Herakles. But they were associated with other tribal peoples and the 'invasion' probably lasted over a period of several generations. There is a general agreement that the immediate origin of the movement was Epeiros and western Macedonia. It is also possible to argue that the first Dorian settlements in the Peloponnese were founded by exiled Achaean leaders and their followers and that the first Dorians in Crete arrived a generation after the Dorian kingdoms had been established in the Peloponnese. But, as we have seen, there is a Homeric tradition that there were Dorians in Crete before the 'Return of the Herakleidai' had begun. Hence the argument that the Dorians invaded by sea, from the Amprakiot Gulf, first to Crete, then to the south Aegean, and finally to the Peloponnese, should not be lightly dismissed, as it sometimes is.

What is certain is that the Dorians, the latest to arrive, most faithfully adhered to their ancient tribal forms of organization and tradition for a long time to come. They were customarily divided into three main groupings. These were: the Hylleis, descended from Hyllos, son of Herakles; the Dymanes, worshipping Apollo; and the Pamphyloi, 'those of all tribes', whose goddess was Demeter. Wherever they subsequently settled, whether on the mainland or overseas, this tribal organization was adapted, at various times and in different places, to the structure of the Iron Age city-state. In the case of Crete it will be necessary to examine this process of adaptation in some detail so far as the evidence will allow.

If, as seems increasingly likely, we accept the tradition that the population of Crete was mixed in origin and that its languages were equally mixed when the Achaeans were at the height of their power in the later Bronze Age, we must also acknowledge that the earliest inscriptional evidence indicates that those whose language was *Doric Greek* had assumed political leadership in the Cretan city-states. The *Cretan dialect*, or, to be more specific, the *Central Cretan* dialect, became the dialect of Gortyn, Knossos, Lyttos, Axos and other cities of central Crete. To the east, in such cities as Olous, Dreros and Lato, we find the dialect to be less uniform in character. At the eastern end of the island, at Hieraptyna, Praisos and Itanos, as also in the western extremity, at Aptera and Kydonia, many characteristics which we regard as peculiarly Cretan were absent. Yet this feature can be explained as the result of external influences, particularly the influences of the *Attic* and *Doric* dialects of the other islands. Therefore it is likely that, if we had more extensive evidence from the earlier period, we should find that the characteristics of the *Central Cretan* dialect were also the characteristics of the *Cretan Doric* dialect in general.[24] Even so, the possiblity of continuing linguistic variety, as the surviving inscriptions in 'Eteocretan' remind us, has to be taken into account.

The details of the Dorian dispersal over Crete and the process of development of Dorian supremacy are not known to us. The kind of evidence which could properly instruct us concerning the phases of the social and economic changes which were brought about in the three hundred years, from approximately

[24] Buck, GD 171-2.

1100 to 800 B.C., remains deficient. From such evidence as there is we can form only general conclusions. When the Achaean hegemony was brought to an end, there appears to have been a quite marked decline in the population of the island. Inland towns and also coastal sites were mainly abandoned and the palace site at Knossos was deserted. By the beginning of the eighth century, however, conditions generally became more settled and some old Minoan sites, including Ayia Triada, Phaistos and Mallia, were again inhabited.

What happened to the majority of the older inhabitants in the social system which eventually became established under the Dorian aristocracies of the historic period remains to be considered. But the system was not speedily brought into being and its process of growth may well have been uneven and diverse in character. For there are reasons for suggesting that the Doric-speaking tribes were ready, or were eventually obliged, to adapt themselves to prevailing conditions, sometimes perhaps to the extent of amalgamating with existing ruling groups. The familiar three Dorian tribal names occur in inscriptions from various cities, but in ten of the cities we find other names in addition, and in two of these the names are of so unusual a kind that the prevalence of non-Dorian elements may have been likely, especially as they occur in the 'Eteocretan' eastern end of the island.[25]

What we do know for certain is that local place-names persisted, since there are few that can be called Doric in origin. It is not unusual that the names of rivers should very often have remained pre-Dorian or pre-Greek. But Hutchinson has suggested, as an explanation of the surprising fact that an overwhelming proportion of the city-names should be pre-Hellenic, the possiblity that the classical population must have been characterized by a large percentage of Minoan blood. For on a map of Hellenistic sites in Crete, he noted twenty-one with modern Greek names, with no known ancient equivalents, eighteen with apparently pre-Hellenic names, three ancient Greek names and two of Venetian origin. Many well-known cities of the historical period have names of Bronze Age origin or earlier, in the west, the centre and the east, including Kydonia, Phalasarna, Sybrita, Rhethymnon, Lappa, Knossos,

[25] Willetts, ASAC 254 n. 1.

Tylisos, Rhaukos, Phaistos, Pyranthos, Lyttos, Eteia and Praisos.[26]

This linguistic persistence was paralleled by a determined effort of some elements of the older population to preserve their independence by taking to the mountains. At such places as Karphi, Vrokastro and Kavousi, cities of refuge were built on commanding heights against the encroachment. The period of occupation of Karphi perhaps lasted from about 1050 to 950 B.C. After about 800 B.C., however, these cities of refuge were either abandoned altogether if they were too inaccessible, or, if their environment was more promising, were developed into city-states. Among the latter was a city whose ancient name is unknown, but which goes by the modern name of the village near its site, Prinias. The hill which formed the centre of this site was first occupied, presumably as a place of refuge, in LM III times. Lato and Axos are two other such cities, which, like Prinias, were not abandoned but grew into city-states.

Since there was this tenacity of tradition among the older population, the Doric-speaking tribal confederacy, though eventually dispersed into many independent city-states, in its turn preserved its common language as a means of perpetuating its own common traditions. No doubt the settlement over all parts of Crete took a long time. It was probably accompanied by conflicts, setbacks, compromises and adjustments about which we can only speculate, since the details of the actual process are obscure. We may fairly safely infer that the Dorians did not arrive in overwhelming numbers, that perhaps in fact their numbers were relatively small. If so there was practical need, in dangerous times, for tribal solidarity to be preserved. Nor were these the only reasons, as we shall see, why Doric speech was so characteristic of historical Crete.

[26] PC 319.

# III

◇◇◇◇◇◇◇◇◇◇◇◇◇◇◇◇◇◇◇◇◇◇◇◇◇◇◇◇◇◇◇◇

## Economic Life

◇◇◇◇◇◇◇◇◇◇◇◇◇◇◇◇◇◇◇◇◇◇◇◇◇◇◇◇◇◇◇◇

CRETE is often rightly enough described as the cradle of European civilization; yet it is modest in size, being no more than about 156 miles long from east to west and about 36 miles from north to south even at its widest point, from Cape Stavros to Cape Kephala. Massive chains of mountains with peaks 8,000 feet high in places, coming very near to the coast in the south, straddle the whole length of the island. To the west are the White Mountains, separated from a second mountain system piled around Mount Ida by a lower, rolling countryside, similar to that which again intervenes before the Dikte massif. Beyond is the flat isthmus of Hierapetra, with the Thriphte mountains to the east, succeeded by a table of limestone as far as the eastern coast. There are fertile plains, like that of Khania on the northwest coast, or the great central plain of Messara in the midsouth. Apart from the low-lying fertile coastal areas, there are upland plains, hilly areas which afford good pasture or arable, and areas higher in the mountains which afford only summer pasturage. But extensive areas have always been unproductive, because they are too high, too wild, too desolate. In the plains the climate is favourably dry, with normal heavy rain in October and in February or March. There is one lake, the 160 acres of Lake Kournas, some eleven miles west of Rhethymnon, in the north-west. There are only five rivers that have never been known to be dry; there are springs in the mountains and wells in the coastal plains.

The seaports of Minoan times were often sited on small promontories, with harbour facilities on both sides according to the direction of the wind. If Homer's account of the Phaiacians in the *Odyssey* is, as some scholars believe, reminiscent of Minoan Crete, then the description of their port of Scherie is in keeping with the identification. For, as Nausicaa explains to Odysseus: 'Around the city is a lofty rampart. There is a fine harbour on each side of it, with a narrow approach-way. Rounded ships are drawn up along the road; and each man has a berth for himself. Here too is their market-place, on both sides of a fair temple of Poseidon, walled with stone blocks, quarried and dragged to the spot, where they tend the tackle of their black ships, cables and sails, and smooth their oars.'[1]

The principal Cretan ports nowadays, Khania, Rhethymnon and Heraklion, are on the north coast. This has not always been the case. In antiquity it was customary to beach ships, whereas now they must have anchorage. Moreover, as Spratt was the first to recognize, in consequence of a geological disturbance in the sixth century A.D., the whole island was raised up in the western part as high as 26 feet above the sea. Hence the harbour of Phalasarna on the west coast now lies about 150 yards inland, well above sea-level. On the other hand, the eastern coastline sank down, allowing the sea to cover sandy beaches on which ships could formerly be drawn up, as well as parts of ancient cities. For example, Mokhlos, now an island, was probably part of the mainland in Minoan times, with two harbours on either side of an isthmus. These changes are at least partly responsible for the major concentration of shipping on the three northern ports.

Even more important in its economic consequences is the wholesale deforestation of Crete which has occurred since antiquity. As Pendlebury remarked, Crete, once one of the most fertile and prosperous islands in the Mediterranean, is now one of the rockiest and most barren.[2] Yet the forests of Crete were still a plentiful source of supply of cypress wood for the Venetian navy in medieval times. In the time of Pliny cypress was even more abundant: now it seems to be restricted to the limestone

[1] *Od. 6.262–9*; Willetts, CCF 127–8.      [2] Pendlebury, AC 6.

area. Ever since men began to live in Crete this steady process of deforestation has been going on; and men have cut down the trees, and have failed to protect young shoots from the ravages of goats.

In Minoan times the whole of Crete west of Ida may well have been covered with forest. As trees disappeared, so the soil which they consolidated was swept by the rains from the hillsides. Half of what forest remains is in the province of Khania, one-fifth on the southern and eastern slopes of the Ida chain.

According to figures for 1948, only 2 per cent of Cretan land was forested. Such crops as wheat, barley and beans accounted for 8 per cent of the total of cultivated land, vines, olives and other fruits for 10 per cent, while 5 per cent was fallow and 7 per cent meadow and grazing land. Of the remainder, 48 per cent was used for nomadic grazing and 20 per cent entirely unproductive in character. If we assume that the area of culti-vated land was roughly the same in antiquity, the most sub-stantial change has been in the very large area which was forested in early times and which is now given up to nomadic grazing.

Still, anyone who has wandered through the towns of Crete at harvest time will have had an impression of ripe abundance. The presumably native quince and almond have been more recently supplemented by apples, peaches, apricots, plums and citrus, just as the prehistoric peas, chickpeas and beans have been supplemented by such vegetables as potatoes. Thirty years ago the then annually increasing crop of shelled almonds averaged 600 tons. Olive trees averaged a yield of 5 lb. of oil, compared with an overall Greek average of 3·7 lb. and 3·1 lb. for Italy and Turkey. The annual crop is in the region of 25,000 tons, much of which is exported to other areas of Greece. Pre-war crops of olives accounted for more than a third of the total Greek crop. Pre-war crops of wheat averaged 12·8 bushels, and of barley 15 bushels per acre. Grapes, mostly in the form of sultanas, are now Crete's largest export, somewhere in the region of 10,000 tons annually. The cultivation of both olives and grapes goes back to the Bronze Age.[3]

There is no evidence so far that Crete was ever inhabited by palaeolithic food-gatherers. But the evidence of neolithic settle-

[3] Hutchinson, PC 41-2.

ment shows that at least the extent if not the density of the area of occupation approximates to that of later Bronze Age times. Usually, however, neolithic settlers avoided the coasts and, in various places, lived in caves rather than in hamlets or villages. But, at Knossos, the ruins of neolithic villages indicate that what was to become the chief centre of Minoan Crete had earlier been the site of one of the largest neolithic settlements of Europe and the Near East. There has been general agreement with Evans's view that neolithic Crete can be regarded as an insular offshoot of an extensive Anatolian province. The first inhabitants of Crete were in fact probably immigrant farmers from Anatolia and the Delta, acquainted with the technical knowledge of their homelands. Hence the first Cretan economy, because it was not indigenous, apparently started at a relatively advanced neolithic level.

The change from palaeolithic food-gathering to neolithic food-production originated in the Near East as a consequence of the climatic conditions following upon the last Ice Age. The grasslands which had covered North Africa and Asia as far as Iran had been reduced. In their place were now areas of desert with fertile oases and river-beds. The descendants of the nomadic tribes who had hunted and gathered their food in the ample grasslands settled down in the more restricted fertile zones to domesticate the animals and cultivate the plants. While the men were still hunters, the women, it seems, began to sow seeds of the wild grasses which became the early strains of wheat and barley. With the breeding of sheep, goats, cattle and pigs, there were continuous supplies of milk and meat, as well as grain. The techniques of pottery, spinning and weaving developed. Dwellings of mud, reeds, logs, stone or withies, plastered with clay, were made with new tools which included the stone axe-head.

The neolithic village economy probably produced a division of labour between the sexes on the following lines. While women cultivated plots of land, ground and cooked grain, spun and wove cloth, made clothes and pottery, their menfolk made weapons and tools, hunted, did the work of building, looked after livestock and cleared new lands for cultivation. As lands were cleared, so the new economy spread. Crete, as a bridgehead in close proximity to Asia, Africa and Europe, must have begun to invite settlers who travelled in primitive boats from the Dodecanese and the Cyclades. As they returned from its coasts, they would reflect on the possibilities afforded by its fertile plains for crops and fruits.

The basic social unit of the palaeolithic peoples was the clan, consolidated by its traditions of kinship and common ownership. The members of a clan were united by descent from an assumed common ancestor, a totem, either animal, plant or natural object. Animals and plants, because they formed the food-supply, were presumably the first kinds of totem, while stones, rain, wind and implements made by man were analogous types conceived later. In a group of blood relatives comprising a clan, intermarriage was not allowed, and the clan was therefore exogamous. Compacts of intermarriage existed between clans, and a group of intermarrying clans united into a wider tribal group. Such a system of intermarriage between clans leads to classificatory systems of relationship, at the same time more involved and more all-embracing than systems of kinship based upon the family as we know it. The clan perpetuated ritual forms of initiatory training, the most familiar of which, to the modern, are the initiation ceremonies of puberty. As we shall see, there were others, parts of a whole protracted cycle, which were no less crucial. The clan could reinforce its members by adopting non-clansmen, provided they were willing to participate in the clan rites.

This basic social system was carried over and developed in neolithic times; and we have to assume that it was an inherited possession of the first settlers in Crete. The system presumably included communal land tenure, since this is a characteristic of modern peoples at a similar stage of social development. Because of its origins, it seems reasonable to assume that Cretan neolithic economy included the cultivation of cereals and fruits, and the breeding of cattle, goats and pigs. However, there may well have been an early and continuing bias in favour of cultivation, promoted by settlement in the fertile lowlands. We shall see that the Gortyn Code indicates a survival of matrilineal institutions into the historical period; and we may fairly assume that these institutions were perpetuated among the older population from early times of settlement in the island. For, although there are many cases of transition from matrilineal to patrilineal descent, it is not possible to cite examples of the reverse process.

Hence the presumption that the former is the earlier. Changes in the division of labour between sexes in primitive society occur as there are changes in modes of production. Women occupy a dominant role in the economy of pure cultivators and descent is matrilineal. But descent is patrilineal among stock-breeders, because men exercise a superior economic and social influence. A temporary priority of matrilineal systems once assumed, a gradual transition from matrilineal to patrilineal systems can be detected. This transition becomes accelerated as stock-raising develops, but is countered in the early phases of agriculture, that is to say when there is garden tillage and not yet field tillage, and before the cattle-drawn plough has replaced the hoe.[4]

The settled village economy established in neolithic times in Crete has been persistent to the extent that, although tools, social organization and religion have undergone successive changes, there still remains the cultivation of some similar crops and the practice of such crafts as spinning, weaving and pottery. Indeed the village must have been relatively little disturbed by the great changes which came about with the development of a Bronze Age economy. But even where these changes operated most decisively, the flexibility and egalitarianism of neolithic tribalism exerted their influence. The palace economy of the middle Bronze Age of Crete developed over a period of about five hundred years with an enterprise which suggests little interference with the basic structure of social life. Thus the very planlessness of Minoan palace architecture, its apparently haphazard, 'cellular' growth, with the addition of structure to structure in varying sizes, have been traced to a similar pattern in the building of neolithic dwellings.

Neolithic economy, we saw, had been transplanted into Crete from the East at a fairly advanced stage. When Bronze Age economy superseded, again the Cretans borrowed from the East, adapting what they borrowed with skilful ingenuity. In the Early Minoan period there was a fresh influx of settlers from Asia and perhaps also from Libya, while trading relations were maintained with Asia, Libya and Egypt. Cretan metal-working began to develop at this time, based upon Eastern traditions which had been very gradually fostered. In the Near and Middle

4 Willetts, CCF 5–7.

East, even assuming that metal-working was widely in vogue soon after 4000 B.C., stone had indeed been slowly abandoned. Bronze implements had mainly succeeded to polished stone celts in Assyria by 3000 B.C., in Egypt by 2000 B.C., but in the Aegean by 1500 B.C.

Specialists such as coppersmiths, goldsmiths, carpenters, jewellers, lapidaries and potters were maintained from the surplus produce of the peasantry by Early Minoan times. Dyeing, fresco-painting and ivory-work made impressive advances. The pivoted disk and the foot-wheel could have been used in Crete by about 1800 B.C. The introduction of the wheel speeded production and, as elsewhere, apparently caused pottery to become an exclusively male occupation. The wheel also revolutionized transport. Solid-wheeled vehicles, known in the East much earlier, were used in Crete round about 2000 B.C. These sufficed for the slow transport of goods. But spoked wheels, attested in northern Mesopotamia and Cappadocia about 2000 B.C., in Egypt soon after 1600 B.C., are represented on Knossian clay tablets about 1500 B.C. The spoked wheel brought speed and easier handling. Not surprisingly, it was soon to produce an efficient instrument of warfare in the form of the war-chariot. Four-spoked wheels were fitted to Mycenaean and Minoan chariots, which may have helped Mycenae to gain its supremacy in the Peloponnese, and Knossos to gain a similar supremacy in Crete in the later Bronze Age.[5]

The centres of the Bronze Age economy were the palaces that were built in such parts of central Crete as Knossos, Phaistos, Mallia, Tylisos and Ayia Triada. These palaces, like Oriental temples, were places of worship in that they had shrines. They were also factories and warehouses, the centres of activity for specialists, dependent upon the palace stores for raw materials. The Bronze Age townships, unplanned, unfortified, developed out of village communities, clustered about the market-places, the original nuclei of settlement.

The Bronze Age 'priest-kings', of whom the legendary Minos of Knossos is the familiar prototype, combined ritualistic with political and social authority. As the whole increasingly complex economy ultimately depended upon the resources of

[5] Lorimer, 322; Evans, PM 4.785ff.; Pendlebury, AC 219; Childe, WHH 147; Willetts, CCF 14–15, 34–5.

agriculture, the regulation of the calendar was of the utmost importance and this duty would naturally devolve upon the 'priest-kings'. With the development of agriculture, the observance of the seasons demands attention. The cycle of the seasons corresponds with the solar astronomical year of 365·24 days. The lunar year of twelve months has 354·36 days. This discrepancy has to be reconciled. When the lunar calendar is periodically reconciled with the solar year by adding a thirteenth month, a lunisolar calendar is introduced. The cycle of intercalation, however, differs. When an extra month is added in nine years out of every twenty-five, as in Egypt, there is a twenty-five-year cycle. In Mesopotamia, the extra month was added in seven years out of nineteen and hence there was a nineteen-year cycle. In Greece the city-states had their own calendars but their structure was uniform. A thirteenth month was intercalated in three years out of every eight, giving an octennial cycle. The evidence suggests that this octennial cycle may have derived from Minoan Crete, where the 'priest-king's' tenure of office is likely to have been restricted to an octennial period.

Long after the Bronze Age kingship and its functions had passed into legend and myth, when republican government was dominant in the Greek city-states, officials continued to be appointed to perform religious offices who clearly derived from the old kings. The 'King' Archon in Athens is a conspicuous example, and, not surprisingly, he had a counterpart who probably exercised similar functions in historical Crete.[6]

All the indications are that, in the Middle Minoan period, Cretan commercial property developed peacefully, without internal strife or threat from overseas, where trading relations were expanded. Commodity production, chiefly of luxury goods, appreciably increased. In fact, a form of money was now required, as revealed by the copper ingots found at Knossos and other sites, which were weighed against other commodities. These trading operations also needed a system of measurement by weights. In order that these operations might be recorded and an inventory of stores maintained, a written script was now also required. Hence the Linear A script, appearing about the middle

[6] Parker, CAE; Neugebauer, 97, 101, 123; L. Bischoff in RE s.v. Kalender; Nilsson, ERBGK, SS, PTR 264; Thomson, SAGS 2.105–127; Willetts, CCF 82–118.

of the seventeenth century B.C., and Linear B, in the course of the fifteenth century B.C., followed upon earlier pictographic scripts.

Since magazines and workshops occupy a relatively large area at Knossos and Phaistos, it has been inferred that a high proportion of their goods was absorbed in trade; and also that the palace economy was based principally upon secondary industry and commerce rather than agricultural products. This would confirm that the social and economic life of the villages, as developed from neolithic times, was not disrupted. Even so, there are important questions that have to be asked, although archaeological remains in themselves cannot supply answers. The expansive economy of the period not only led to the construction of great palaces but also of harbours, bridges, roads and aqueducts. We should like to know how the labour force necessary for these immense tasks was supplied. We may suppose that at least domestic slavery had been instituted in the palace households. But it is much more difficult to imagine a labour force of slaves in sufficient numbers for the construction and maintenance of palaces and public works. A more likely solution is that the peasantry of the surrounding villages were obliged to contribute labour services for such purposes at specified periods.

We have also to conjecture whether a surplus of such products as wine and oil, destined for export, was exchanged in the market for wares supplied by merchants, or whether such a surplus became available to merchants as a form of tribute imposed and assessed by the palaces. In other words, we are not yet in a position to decide whether tributary relations had modified the communal relations surviving from neolithic times by the Middle Minoan period. We are on safer ground, however, in suggesting that such kinds of tribute and services had become general by the Late Bronze Age, and certainly by the time the Achaeans were exercising their supremacy. For Bronze Age economy of the later second millennium B.C., whether among Hittites, Egyptians and Achaeans, or among contemporary Chinese, shares certain general characteristics of militarization, social inequalities accompanied by rigid divisions of labour, including a large class of farmers rendering tribute and also services to a central authority.

This growth of social inequality was stimulated by concentration of wealth in the hands of ruling groups who controlled the technical resources of Bronze Age economy. Bronze was expensive because it was not abundant; and it was essential in the manufacture of commodities which primarily benefited the wealthy minority who had a monopoly control of its supply. A surplus from the peasantry was necessary to maintain the increasing numbers of specialist craftsmen. The wares produced by the latter were handled and exchanged by another class of specialists, the merchants. This centralized economy could benefit only the wealthy minority and merchants, craftsmen, administrators, soldiers. The cultivators could not benefit from an expanding circulation of luxury commodities.

When the rulers of these lop-sided economies began to extend their system to other territories by conquest and diplomacy, they prepared its downfall. Decay of the Bronze Age societies of the Mediterranean had become general by about 1200 B.C. Wealth had been concentrated in restricted sectors and could not be used to promote technical advances to benefit the whole. Instead, the techniques were applied to warfare. In consequence, it is agreed that Mycenaean society becomes progressively impoverished in the late fourteenth and in the thirteenth centuries B.C. Its eventual collapse, with the arrival of the Dorians, had been prepared for by its nature, by the very process of its development.

The development of bronze-working is the central feature of Middle Minoan times. Older Bronze Age societies of the Near East had depended upon the techniques of pottery, spinning and weaving, the smelting and casting of copper, manufacture of bronze from copper and tin, the plough, the wheeled cart, the harness and the sailing-ship, followed, early in the third millennium B.C., by the bellows, the tongs and the *cire-perdue* process of bronze-casting. In Egypt and Mesopotamia, irrigation too had played a vital part in the large-scale agriculture which produced a vast surplus appropriated by the ruling classes. This surplus was used partly for producing commodities. In Mesopotamia even a rudimentary system of silver money came into use. But commodity production in Mesopotamia was chiefly restricted to luxury articles. Therefore, there remained a basic internal natural economy, even though part of the agricultural

45

surplus was being exchanged for raw materials. The need for such raw materials as metals and timber, exacted as tribute or exchanged for foodstuffs and luxury articles, caused the Mesopotamian cities to expand. Trading relations were maintained not only with Egypt and Anatolia but extended to the coasts of Syria and Palestine, where another group of city-states arose, with good harbours, adjacent to fertile valleys and to mountains with ample supplies of timber, stone and tin. Less dependent on centralized irrigation, they could produce less of an agricultural surplus. Industrial production was, however, more intense, with the manufacture of luxury goods like jewellery and cosmetics, with dye-works, copper-foundries, workshops for the making of bronze tools, and shipyards.

The city of Ugarit (Ras Shamra) was one such thriving port, at its most flourishing from 1800 to 1200 B.C. Here the wares of Syria and of the Hittites were exchanged with those of Egypt and Cyprus, Knossos and, later, Mycenae. The prosperity of such cities rested upon the carrying trade and therefore upon the accumulation of merchants' capital. The craftsmen specialists of these cities were members of fraternities or guilds. The Ugaritic evidence shows that they were often categorized according to hereditary occupations, including warriors and priests of various kinds, smiths, builders, wainwrights, potters, launderers, sculptors, fowlers, shepherds, grooms, gatekeepers. Taxes and dues were exacted in silver, by labour service or in kind. Military and naval manpower was made available to the state through draft quotas on the communities and guilds. Obligations to the state, as well as benefits provided by the state, were administered through town-districts, but also partly by the guilds. Developments of this kind encroached upon, but did not entirely disrupt, the old tribal system. Though names were more commonly qualified by those of their local township, the older habit of qualification by tribal name still sometimes persisted. Members of the king's clan and other politically privileged clans held such important offices as the priesthood.[7]

After the initial technical advances mentioned above, there was a marked slowing down in the later third millennium B.C. and the stagnation remains until the end of the Bronze Age. There were no wheeled ploughs, though both wheel and plough

[7] Gordon, UL 122-6.

were in use. It was not until the early Middle Ages that the harness, used for oxen in the Bronze Age, was adapted for horses; and there was a similar time-lag before the rudder replaced the steering-oar. It has been observed that these improvements were not made, because there was an ample supply of cheap human labour, as communal relations among the peasantry became transformed into tributary relations. If we suppose that the great public works of the Bronze Age were executed by the labour services of peasants, this is not to deny that slavery existed, especially in the temples, but the role of slavery in Bronze Age economies, though difficult to assess, was probably by no means decisive.

The Cretan Bronze Age cities, contemporary with the Syrian, shared many of their characteristics, not only in the purely technical field, but in other ways, such as, in all probability, the exacting of labour services from the peasantry, the levying of tributes of various kinds, and the organization of craftsmen into guilds. Such tendencies are certainly confirmed by later Greek tradition. The prestige of the Bronze Age Cretan craftsman, for example, is reflected in the legends about Daidalos ('the cunning worker', 'the artist'), the mythical prototype of Greek sculptors.

There was also an abiding tradition about the nature of the Bronze Age Cretan social organization and its similarity to the Egyptian. Aristotle tells us that the 'caste-system' still prevalent in the Egypt and Crete of his own times was established in Crete by Minos, and in Egypt by Sesostris. He thus reminds us of its ancient Bronze Age origins when he is explaining that it was not an original or a recent discovery of political philosophy that a state should be divided into 'castes' or 'classes'; that warriors should be distinguished from farmers. The Greek word for 'caste' is *genos*, whose basic meaning is 'kin'. It is also the common word for 'clan'. A similar terminology was used in other accounts of the Egyptian social system. Herodotos says that the Egyptians were divided into the seven 'castes' of priests, warriors, cowherds, swineherds, tradesmen, interpreters, boatmen. Diodoros, like Aristotle, stresses the antiquity of the Egyptian system and states that the country was divided into three parts, the first allotment going to the priestly hierarchy, the second to the kings, the third to the warriors. He adds that there were three other 'orders' in the state, herdsmen, cultivators, artisans. The cultivators rented the arable land held by the king, priests and warriors, and devoted their time to farming. Nor were the craftsmen allowed to follow any other craft than their own.[8]

Such traditions indicate the ways in which the old tribal system of neolithic times could have been modified by the economic system of the Bronze Age. Archaeological evidence also indicates changes. The standard Minoan burial custom was collective interment in caves, stone chambers, or *tholos* tombs—communal burial places too large for a family but large enough for a clan. In some places grouping of the graves indicates the association of several kindreds in a single village settlement. However, individual interment in stone cists, jars and clay coffins began before the end of Early Minoan and steadily increased later. This process has been taken to imply the disintegration of the clan. On the other hand, jar burials may be exceptional in the sense that many could have been used for infants; and individual interment in any case did not become standard. Therefore it may be safe to conclude that the old tribal institutions were, as at Ugarit, certainly modified and adapted but by no means completely disrupted even in urban or palace areas. In remoter areas there was perhaps little basic change. As we shall see, the *oikos*, the 'household', which preserved, albeit in restricted fashion, the collective customs of the clan, was of considerable importance in the Cretan society of the historical period. The 'household', like the 'caste system' and the tribal system, may have been a Bronze Age legacy perpetuated and adapted by later Dorian rulers.[9]

In fact such survivals testify to that tenacity of tribal institutions which is a feature of ancient Greek society as a whole until well into the historical period. The use of the term 'guild' for the fraternities or 'castes' with special functions in the Bronze Age evokes comparison with the medieval guilds. Such comparison is more than superficial. For the medieval guild was very similar to the craft or occupational clans which developed within the higher grades of tribal society as a means of transmitting

[8] Arist. *Pol.* 1329 a 40–1329 b 5; Hdt. 2.164–8; D.S.I. 73–4.
[9] Childe, DEC 22–4; Evans, PM 1.70–2, 149–50; Hall, CGBA 44; Willetts, ASAC 29, 59–63, 65, 252–3, 255, CCF 20–1.

hereditary occupations. In ancient Greece these 'guilds' were even closer to their tribal origin. Thus the Asklepiadai (physicians) traced their ancestry to the patron of medicine, Asklepios (whose cult, incidentally, was prominent in Crete in historical times, especially at the port of Gortyn, Lebena). Similarly, the Homeridai (minstrels) claimed descent from Homer. The Iamidai (prophets), represented in Elis, Sparta, Messenia and Kroton, derived from a son of Apollo, the god of prophecy. Other prophets were the Branchidai and Krontidai. The Kerykes, Theokerykes and Talthybiadai were all heralds, the former deriving from a son of Hermes, the god of heraldry, the others from the herald Talthybios. All heralds in Sparta were Talthybiadai, since heraldry was their clan-prerogative. There were other craft-clans with vocational names, such as Poimenidai (herdsmen), Bouzygai (ox-spanners), Phreorychoi (well-diggers), Daidalidai (sculptors), Hephaistiadai, Eupyridai and Pelekes (armourers and smiths). A mythical division of labour among the deities of Olympos was a religious counterpart of this system of occupational clans, which determined a man's calling according to the clan into which he was born. Zeus became king as a reward for military service against Kronos and the Titans. He was then in a position to distribute spheres of influence to other deities: to Hephaistos, fire; to Atlas, support of the sky; to Apollo, music and dancing; to Hades, lamentation and darkness; to Aphrodite, love-making; to Athene, the loom; to Poseidon, the sea; to himself, the sky.[10]

There is need to emphasize the legacies of the Bronze Age where, as in Crete, they abided in strength, because, in general, the Greek institutions of the first millennium B.C., with the onset of the Iron Age, are too often represented in their novelty. But this novelty is sharpened, rather than diminished, when it is seen in more balanced historical perspective.

The first fundamental development of the Iron Age is, of course, the increasing use of iron as a basic metal. The smelting of iron is a craft thought to have been discovered in Armenia. Though known to the Hittites, it was not widely practised by them. Iron-working in Iran, Transcaucasia, Syria and Palestine had grown rapidly between 1200 and 1000 B.C., and Cyprus, Caucasia and Crete were not far behind these other centres. New

[10] Grönbech, 1.35; Thomson, SAGS I² 332–4.

processes enabling steel to become at least equal, if not superior, to bronze had followed in all these areas the earlier iron-smelting. Therefore the smelting of iron was to spread much more quickly than had the smelting of bronze. Even so, several centuries were required for the diffusion and firm foundation of the new techniques, until Greece in general can be said to have emerged fully into the Iron Age round the about middle of the eighth century B.C. Although rings and other ornaments of iron appeared in Mycenaean times and in sub-Mycenaean graves, it was the Protogeometric period which in Athens coincided with its increasingly common use. Still a precious metal in the sub-Mycenaean period, iron became normally used for weapons from Early Protogeometric times onward. But iron weapons found in Crete belong to an earlier date than Cretan Protogeometric and may even antedate Attic Protogeometric. However, down to the middle of the eighth century B.C., copper and stone were still most commonly used for tools in Greece, partly, it has been argued, because the Aegean was still too poor to support a large iron trade, partly because Greece itself was relatively weak in native ores of iron. Thus while iron gradually replaced bronze as the chief metal, in Crete fine work continued to be done in bronze, including several important works of art. In fact, it is agreed that Cretan metallurgy in the archaic period was one of the most developed in the whole of Greece, because it was continuing a very ancient tradition.

Since it needs higher temperatures, iron-smelting presented more difficulty than copper-smelting. But it was more widely available and therefore cheaper. Once the new techniques had been developed, iron became a superior basic metal to bronze and copper. Unlike the rarer bronze, which had been mainly used for weapons and luxury articles, the new metal was of widespread practical value because it could be made into axes and hammers, knives, sickles and ploughshares for general use. The consequences were revolutionary. Hitherto Bronze Age agriculture had been able to provide a surplus to maintain craftsmen, but craftsmen's products had benefited a minority. Now, with, the spread of iron-working, domestic industry could be attached to agriculture. Craftsmen's products could become available to farmers who could thus increase their productivity. The balanced relationship now achieved for the first time between agriculture and industry could lead to a self-sufficiency of village producers independent of such a wide market as had formerly characterized the Aegean Bronze Age. Eventually that market was to be re-established, as the economy of the city-states matured, but on a radically new basis, correlated with the new stage in the expansion of commodity production which was stimulated by the introduction of iron-working.[11]

The political form of the new economy was the city-state. By the development of the city-state in its classical form, the old village commune, with its traditions of common ownership, was to be changed into a community of peasant proprietors, engaged in independent production for the market. However, this process was far from uniform. The peasant proprietors of Athens achieved their status after protracted class struggles culminating in a democratic revolution. The peasants of historical Crete never achieved their independence. In Crete, the traditions of common ownership based on the village commune were joined to a system of tributary exaction which the Dorian aristocracies durably consolidated.

The initial development of the Iron Age in Crete seems to have been accompanied by an intensification of collective traditions at various levels. We have seen how the old population in some cases maintained itself for a time in hardy isolation in its mountain refuges. Elsewhere, the Dorian newcomers, apparently either in association with existing ruling groups, or independently, established themselves as aristocratic minorities, appropriating the land and its cultivators alike as instruments of production. A form of land tenure thus developed which was based on the inherited Minoan-Mycenaean, as modified by Doric, tribalism. The Bronze Age 'caste system' was taken over by new masters with new techniques. The cultivators became vassals, serfs. Dorian supremacy was achieved through the exactions of a tributary system imposed upon surviving forms of the primitive village commune.

We must trace, in later chapters, the outlines of this aristocratic system as it emerges into the light of history. We must also examine the slow, halting process of its disintegration, which can be illustrated fairly clearly in the case of Crete,

[11] Forbes in Singer, 595; Pendlebury, AC 336; Desborough, PG 288, 301–2, cf. 252, 255; Willetts, CCF 38.

because there were no explosive political changes of the kind which elsewhere established new forms in place of old to dominate the historical scene.

However, some mention must first be made of the other general developments of the Iron Age which, apart from iron-working, also influenced Crete. These are the growth of trade, the invention of the coinage, and the expansion of chattel slavery.

In the earlier period preceding the Persian Wars, expanding Greek trade was centred upon a number of geographically suit-able commercial points. These included Corinth, Aigina and Athens in Greece itself; Miletos in Asia Minor, to serve the carrying trade between Asia Minor and the Mediterranean; Naukratis in Egypt, to serve a similar purpose for Egypt and the Mediterranean; and Carthage and Massilia (Marseille) in the west. The chief commodities exchanged were apparently not articles of common use. They mainly consisted of gold, ivory, silver, expensive metal-work and vases, woven cloths, orna-ments. Most important of all was the traffic in slaves. The traders presumably not only carried finished goods, but oil and wine and such raw materials as iron, tin, purple, timber. There are certain indications that Crete was affected by this commercial enterprise.

First, we can point to such general features as the early development of alphabetic writing leading to a correspondingly early practice of written law. These developments occurred after the Dorians had resumed the Cretan tradition of urbanization with a zeal that contrasts markedly with the relatively slow development of towns by their kinsfolk on the mainland. But tradition could not of itself have been responsible for early Cretan Doric urbanization. As Pendlebury noted, the true Hellenic period in Crete begins with the eighth century B.C. There was either a westward drift of population or, more prob-ably, settlement of the west by immigrants from the mainland. The great cities of Axos, Polyrhenia and Hyrtakina were founded, and excavation might show that other cities like Phalasarna, Elyros and Sybrita have remains of this period. There were only slightly smaller new foundations at Rhokka, Bene and Ornithe; and Eleutherna and Kydonia rapidly ex-panded. Of course there was the stimulus of new growth promoted by the now more stable social system based on Iron Age techniques. But there was also a stimulus derived from contact overseas.[12]

Our knowledge of artefacts of the Late Geometric period (770–735 B.C., on Brock's dating) is largely derived from family chamber tombs excavated near Knossos and by some finds at Arkhades. Some of the small flasks were either imports from Cyprus or Cretan imitations of such imports. Late Geometric vases were also imported from Attica and the Cyclades. The period from 735 to 680 B.C. is termed by Brock significantly as the Early Orientalizing period. Decorative motifs of oriental origin appeared on native vases near Knossos, and new vase shapes made their appearance, borrowed from Cyprus or the Greek mainland. The famous bronze shields found in the Idaian cave were also influenced from the east. One type of shield is known from all over Europe in the eighth and seventh centuries B.C., in Ireland, Spain, Germany, Bohemia, Italy, Greece and Cyprus, as well as Crete. Hutchinson has pointed out that at least three of the Greek examples were found at Panhellenic sanctuaries, and that examples from other parts of Europe may well be related to the trade routes by which amber from the Baltic was distributed. For Cretan graves of the period sometimes contain amber beads or jewels with inlaid amber. Ivories from the Idaian cave were imported from Syria and Phoenicia. Throughout the eighth and seventh centuries B.C., the Cretan plastic arts of sculpture, modelling and carving in stone, clay, bronze, gold and ivory flourished.[13]

Egyptian scarabs and beads of faience appear in tombs of the Late Orientalizing period (680–635 B.C.) and indicate a renewal of contact with Egypt. Egyptian influence has also been detected in the Cretan sculpture of this time. Vases were imported from Cyprus, Corinth, the Cyclades and Athens and were imitated by Cretan potters. Not that the potters had to rely upon imitation to produce good work. Of some vases found at Arkhades in tombs of this period, Hutchinson says that they were the products of a very lively and original peasant art, often quite prolific in ideas and fancies, less sophisticated than those of Knossos but also more original.[14]

---

[12] Pendlebury, AC 327; Willetts, ASAC 250–1.
[13] Hutchinson, PC 333–9.      [14] *Ibid.*, 347.

Thus the commercial expansion of the early Iron Age did have a generally stimulating effect upon the Cretan aristocracies. The development of trade was presumably controlled by the aristocracies and kept within limits. There was to be no rise of a merchant class on a significant scale.

The success of the Cretan aristocracies in so long keeping trade within safe limits may be judged from the growth of the Cretan coinage. Before the invention of the coinage, trade had been dependent upon barter or upon the use of articles of iron, gold and silver as a medium of exchange. To facilitate commercial expansion, the coinage was invented. It was a brilliant invention. At once a medium was available which was light in weight, standard in value and guaranteed by the authority of a state. Previous devices were clumsy in comparison, a fetter upon the circulation of commodities. Greek society was the first to be based upon a monetary economy. The significance of this development, as Thomson has remarked, has seldom been appreciated. According to Greek tradition, the first coins were invented by the kings of Lydia. From Lydia the new medium spread to the cities of Ionia, then across the Aegean to Aigina, Euboia, Corinth, Athens and then to the Greek cities in Italy and Sicily. Thenceforth commodity production and exchange could develop and capital be accumulated without the inhibition of simple barter or bulky rudimentary forms of money.[15]

But Cretan coinage did not develop until the beginning of the fifth century B.C., that is to say, about 150 years after the earliest adoption of a coinage by a European Greek state, the island of Aigina. But in contrast, we should remember that just as Dorian Sparta did not codify law, so its aristocratic rulers were equally reluctant to encourage trade and private property. For the Spartans had no coinage of their own—aside from the traditional iron money—until metal coins began to be struck at Sparta in the third century B.C.

The usual Cretan standard was, in the Classical period, the Aiginetic, the chief denominations being the stater or didrachm and the drachma. After the time of Alexander, the Attic standard gradually replaced the Aiginetic. After 200 B.C., many cities struck imitations of the Athenian tetradrachm with their own names and symbols. Gortyn was among the first of the Cretan

[15] Thomson, SAGS 2.194–6; cf. Engels, OF 125.

1. Knossos (showing Bull Fresco).

2. Ayia Triada (near Phaistos).

cities to have a coinage. The other cities to issue a coinage during the first period of development from about 500 to about 430 B.C. were Phaistos, Knossos, Itanos, Eleutherna, Lyttos, and Praisos. After 430 B.C., other cities began to issue a coinage. Until autonomous issues ceased after the Roman conquest, we know for certain that nearly forty cities of Crete had a coinage; and several of the cities produced coins which are admired as outstanding examples of the coin-engraver's art. The introduction of Cretan coinage antedates, so far as our present knowledge goes, the publication of the Gortyn Code by about one generation. We are thus obliged to recognize a connexion between trade, coinage and written law. Moreover, just because the Gortyn Code was published at this time, we are in a position to assess some of the immediate consequences of the penetration of a money economy, with its implications for the future development of private property, into the fabric of one sector of ancient Greek society.

During the two centuries which preceded the Persian Wars there were a few innovations to be added to the store of techniques inherited from Bronze Age economy. These were the sheep-shears, the rotary quern, the wine-press and the crane. No other inventions before the Hellenistic age are on record. Technical improvement was hampered by the growth of chattel slavery on a massive scale from the fifth century B.C. onward. For instance, it is significant, with regard to the limitations of ancient democracy we noticed earlier (p. 7), that Chios was the first Greek city to employ chattel slaves; and that this island had a democratic constitution as early as 600 B.C.[16] Crete retained its aristocratic institutions and none of its cities, so far as we know, ever had democratic constitutions. Hence chattel slavery was slow to penetrate into the economy. Again the Cretan evidence forces upon us a sharp contrast between tenacious older social forms and lately emergent new forms. For in Crete in the fifth century B.C. the foundation of the economy is a kind of servitude distinct from chattel slavery. Because it is distinct, it deserves to be called by a distinctive name—either patriarchal slavery or serfdom.

[16] Lilley, 28; Thomson, SAGS 2.197; Tod, 1.2.

# IV

<hr style="border: dotted;" />

# The City-states and their Government

<hr style="border: dotted;" />

For Homer, Crete was traditionally an island with ninety or a hundred cities. Archaeological investigation increasingly confirms this tradition of urbanization; and the student of the institutions of historical Crete already has at his disposal epigraphical material from about sixty cities from the mid-seventh century B.C. onward. The extent to which these institutions survived in modified forms from the Bronze Age can only be partially assessed until we have more information of various kinds. Modern historians, especially those who have accepted the proposed decipherment of the Linear B script, are sometimes prone to oversimplify the contrast between Minoan and Hellenic. On the one hand they depict a late Bronze Age bureaucracy centred upon Knossos, fantastic in its proportions, in the degree of its detailed control of the economic and social life of the period; on the other, a slow resumption of civilized life in quite new forms after a 'dark age'. The supremacy of Knossos in the later Bronze Age is a reasonable inference from the archaeological and the later literary evidence. We cannot, however, define the supremacy because we do not know the area which Knossos directly or indirectly controlled. Archaeology can tell us much about Minoan palaces and towns, but little so far about villages and hamlets, about the way of life of the majority of the population. The evidence is partial and should be treated accordingly.

We know little about the functions of the Minoan 'priest-king'. What we do know or can infer leads us to suppose that he was not an Oriental despot. Nor was he a god incarnate like some of his Oriental counterparts. Even so, his sacral role appears to have been more prominent than his political role. The very planlessness of the Minoan towns indicates a flexibility in social relations that can be interpreted as due to the vigorous survival of tribal institutions, less modified in Crete by urbanization than in either Mesopotamia or Egypt. The Minoan towns have no temples. They are centred around a market-place. In fact, some recent excavations at Mallia indicate that, early in the second millennium (c. 1800 B.C.), the town had, in addition to its palace, a market-place and also a civic building of some kind. Hence there may now be clearer evidence for the view that Bronze Age Cretan cities were not centres of theocratic domination; rather, that assemblies of citizen representatives of some sort were regularly convened for purposes of public business. Indeed it has been suggested that there is a direct line of descent from the juxtaposed palace–market-place–town-hall of Mallia to the temple–market-place–town-hall combination of the city-states of historical times.[1]

The early revival of urbanization in Dorian Crete certainly supports some such inference. The Late Minoan city of refuge called Prinias (after the modern nearby village of that name) was sited on a hill, which overlooks the road from Heraklion to the Messara Plain. It was not abandoned in the archaic period. Two temples have been excavated, one of which dates to c. mid-seventh century B.C.; some of its features have been cited as more reminiscent of the small shrines of the Late Minoan III period than of the archaic Greek temple.

Even more important in this connexion is the site of Lato in the East of Crete, because it conveys an excellent impression of the main features of an early city of the Dorian period. It is likely that Lato commanded the neighbouring plain of Lakonia and the coast routes by the eighth century B.C., as well as a secondary harbour town (Lato pros Kamara or 'Lato-at-the-Arch', the modern Ayios Nikolaos). Lato had a steep double acropolis, a market-place (*agora*) and a town-hall (*prytaneion*) approached by a flight of steps, a temple and other public buildings

[1] Van Effenterre, VPPPM.

which, though on a simple scale, yet formed the centre of the city. Not far to the north of Lato lies Dreros, another archaic city with the same features of *agora*, *prytaneion* and temple, whose remains date back to the eighth century B.C.

Actual evidence relating to the early phases of the political system established in the Cretan city-states is slight. According to Aristotle,[2] though there was monarchy in early times, it was subsequently abolished. Herodotus[3] certainly mentions a king by the name of Etearchos who ruled in the city of Axos; and the word for king has been deciphered in an inscription from Lappa, perhaps of the early fifth century B.C. Such is the extent of the evidence. The context of Aristotle's testimony is, however, significant. For he states that the former military leadership of the kings had now been taken over by the ruling magistrates, the *kosmoi*. Hence we can infer that the tribal chieftains who led the Dorians over Crete enjoyed powers of royal leadership sanctioned by their warrior rank-and-file. A conquering minority in troubled times, they would have been determined to maintain their superiority by force of arms.

We probably have an insight into somewhat similar general conditions in earlier Achaean times from Homer. For Odysseus, on his return to Ithaca, represents himself as a petty Cretan chieftain who refused to serve under Idomeneus at Troy, maintained personal command over his own troops, and subsequently killed the king's son who tried to rob him of the spoils of war.[4]

Only a firm central authority could have prevented the repetition of such episodes. They must have been frequent enough in post-Minoan times, before Dorian rule was secure. The Iron Age was to see the establishment of small, separate communities, and therefore a strict delimitation of the area in which central authority could be established. Wherever it was established, the monarchies developed on a tribal basis in response to the needs of warfare did not survive into the historical period of the city-states. In Sparta, by contrast, the system of dual monarchy was perpetuated as a part of the Dorian aristocratic régime. Sparta itself, even in the time of Thucydides, remained a cluster of villages rather than a compact city.[5] In Crete the system took early root in many dispersed areas where cities were no novelty. The aristocrats, once established in the cities,

[2] *Pol.* 1272 a 9–11.   [3] 4.154.   [4] *Od.* 13.256 ff.   [5] Thuc. 1.10.2.

could manage war as they could manage everything else, without a king. The Spartan and the Cretan systems have much in common. But in several decisive fields—urbanization, the abolition of monarchy, the introduction of coinage and the codification of law—the Cretan has to be sharply distinguished from the Spartan form of aristocratic government.

There were three principal political bodies responsible for managing the affairs of the aristocratic city-states of Crete. By far the most important of these bodies was that composed of the *kosmoi*, as the chief officials were called. This body was also referred to by the collective name of the *kosmos*. The word *kosmos* means 'order' as well as 'ruler'. Its verbal cognate *kosmeo* is used by Homer in the *Iliad* of settling tribes in occupied territory or of marshalling by tribes and phratries for war: it harks back to a time when tribal institutions have been adapted to warfare. The 'order' imposed on Cretan society by its Dorian aristocratic rulers is aptly commemorated by this application of a tribal name to a state functionary. For, in the very process of settlement in Crete, the Dorian tribal system became converted into an apparatus of state. Henceforth the Cretan cities formed a social 'order'. The early Ionian philosophers pictured the world in rather similar terms. For to them *kosmos* signified 'world order'.

In addition to their *kosmoi*, the city states also had their regular Councils and Assemblies. The literary authorities of the fourth century B.C. describe these constitutional bodies when the system had reached a stage of maturity and indeed when it was already affected by the onset of prolonged crisis.

Something of what the fourth-century historian Ephoros had to say about Crete survives in the much later writings of Strabo.[6] Ephoros is reported as disagreeing with the opinion expressed by other writers that most Cretan institutions are Spartan: the truth being that they were invented by the Cretans and only perfected by the Spartans. The Cretans, however, when their cities, and especially Knossos, entered upon troubled times, neglected military affairs. Hence some of their old institutions survive to a greater extent among the Lyttians, Gortynians and some other smaller states than among the Knossians. Many Spartan institutions are called 'Cretan' among the

[6] Str. 10.480–4.

Spartans, as if they originated in Crete. Some of the public offices are not only administered in the same way as in Crete but have the same names, for example, the *Gerontes* (Senators) and the *Hippeis* (Knights). (The supposition that the first of these names was Cretan was presumably due to a confusion with Spartan terminology. The Knights are otherwise unknown to us. Perhaps they existed as an aristocratic, military sect in the time of Ephoros and later became of less account.)

The Spartan ephors, Ephoros continues, have the same function as the Cretan *kosmoi*, although they have different names. He adds that the Cretans choose ten of these magistrates; in affairs of greatest importance they employ as counsellors what they call Senators (*Gerontes*); and those who have been deemed worthy to hold the office of the *kosmoi* and are otherwise thought to be worthy men are appointed members of this Council. In conclusion, Strabo says that he has assumed the Cretan constitution to be worth describing on account both of its peculiar nature and of its reputation. However, not many of the institutions survive, since the administration of affairs in his day was carried out by means of the decrees of the Romans, as in other provinces.

Aristotle deals with Crete in the 2nd book of his *Politics*. His initial discussion of constitutional matters recalls what Ephoros has to say. The Cretan form of constitution, according to Aristotle, approximates to the Spartan. Though in a few particulars not inferior, it is, generally speaking, less polished. The Spartan constitution appears, and is actually said to have been copied in most particulars from the Cretan—illustrating a general truism that the old is less perfected than the new. Aristotle also records the tradition that Spartan institutions are not Dorian, but pre-Dorian, established in Crete first of all by Minos, then taken over from the previous inhabitants by the Spartan colony of Lyttos, whence they were passed to the Spartan lawgiver Lykourgos, when he visited Crete. Hence the laws of Minos are still in force among the subject population of Crete.

He then goes on to specify the resemblances between Sparta and Crete. The land in Sparta is cultivated by helots, in Crete by serfs. Both Sparta and Crete have *syssitia* ('common meals', 'dining-halls'). That these originated in Crete is proved because their old Spartan name was not *pheiditia* but *andreia* ('men's houses'), as in Crete. The same is true of the constitution: the Spartan ephors have the same power as the Cretan *kosmoi*. But there are five ephors in Sparta, ten *kosmoi* in Crete. The *Gerontes* (Senators) at Sparta are the same as the Senators called by the Cretans *Boule* (Council). Elsewhere in his *Politics* Aristotle points out that *Boule* means the Council of a democratic city-state. Therefore his comparison here between Cretan *Boule* and Spartan *Gerontes* illustrates the survival of a more archaic, aristocratic role. Its function in the constitution is clarified by Aristotle's statement elsewhere in the *Politics*[7] that the magistracy which convenes the sovereign Assembly is the sovereign power in the state.

Having still in mind a comparison with Sparta, Aristotle then inserts his remarks about the early existence of monarchy and its later abolition by the Cretans, with the *kosmoi* assuming leadership in war. All, he informs us, participate in the Assembly, whose powers are limited to the ratification of measures decided upon by Senators and *kosmoi*.

The regulations about the Cretan *kosmoi* he considered inferior to those concerning the Spartan ephors. Because in both cases the offices are filled by chance persons, there is a similar constitutional fault. However, the office confers certain advantages upon the Spartan constitution which do not operate in Crete. The ephors are appointed from the general citizen body. Hence the Spartan people have an interest in the preservation of the constitution because of this share in the highest office. In Crete, however, the *kosmoi* are not chosen from the whole people, but from certain clans.

The Senators are chosen from those who have held the office of *kosmos*. (Aristotle's evidence here does not entitle us to assume that ex-*kosmoi* became life-members of the Council automatically.) The Cretan system can be criticized on the same grounds as the Spartan. Members of the Council are given a more exalted postition than they deserve because of their life-tenure of office and freedom from being called to account. Administration of office at their own discretion, without the guidance of written rules, is dangerous. It is not necessarily a sign of a good constitution that the people quietly suffer their exclusion. For, unlike the ephors, the *kosmoi* do not stand to profit from their

[7] 1322 b 15.

office, as they live in an island, remote from people who might corrupt them. Also, they have a curious remedy, more dynastic than constitutional, against the defect of the undue restriction of the office. For *kosmoi* are often overthrown by conspiracies either of their own colleagues or of private citizens. The *kosmoi* too can also resign during their term of office.

It would be better, in Aristotle's opinion, for such safeguards to be enforced by law rather than through men's caprice, an unsafe kind of expedient. But the worst device of all is the suspension of the office of *kosmoi*, often brought about by powerful people to escape justice. Though such a suspension does illustrate that there is a constitutional element operating in the system, this would be better described, however, not as constitutional so much as cabalistic. To form divisions among the people and among friends is nothing unusual, with the consequent abandonment of lawful government through factions and fighting among themselves, the temporary collapse of state authority and a dissolving of the bonds of civil society. States where such things can happen are bound to be insecure, when those who wish are also able to attack them. However, Crete is saved by its geographic location, since distance produces the same effects as acts restricting aliens. (In many Greek states, especially where trade and industry were developed, resident aliens were an important element in the community. Sparta was economically self-sufficient in comparison and foreigners were tolerated only in special circumstances and could be banished by the ephors for undesirable behaviour. Aristotle is arguing that geography does for Crete what conscious policy does for Sparta.) In the same way, the Cretan serf-population stays undisturbed, but the Spartan helots often revolt. For the Cretans have no foreign dominion and, moreover, the island has only recently been invaded by warfare from abroad, which has brought into the open the weakness of its prevailing laws.

The precise meaning of Aristotle's reference to an invasion of warfare from abroad is disputed. It may be that he is recalling the event of 343 B.C., when the Phocian Phalaikos came to Crete with mercenary troops and served with Knossos against Lyttos, or another war ten years later. Whatever the date, Aristotle thought the event of major significance, signifying the onset of crisis in the whole Cretan system.

Aristotle's opinion was that the laws in most cities of his time were in a state of general confusion. Nevertheless, where they could be said to have some definite object in view, that object was always mastery, as in Sparta and Crete, where the educational system and the laws for the most part were shaped with a view to war. These remarks occur in Book 7 of the *Politics*.[8]

Later in this same book[9] he goes on to consider the composition of the whole community in the best kind of constitution. The citizens, he considers, should not be artisans or traders: the life of such people is ignoble and hostile to virtue; nor should they be farmers, because leisure is needed for the generaton of virtue and for political activities. Because the state also has a military section and a section that is concerned with policy-matters and with justice (these being parts of the state in a special sense), Aristotle asks whether these sections are to be regarded as distinct or whether both types of function are to be carried out by the same people. His answer is that both should be done by the same people, but not at the same time. For those who possess arms have the power to decide whether the constitution stands or falls. Hence the two functions should go to the same people, but according to the order of nature, younger men having strength and older men wisdom.

The same kind of people, continues Aristotle, should own property. For they are the citizens, and the citizens ought to be well provided. Whereas the artisan class has no part in the state, nor any other class which is not involved in the craft of virtue. It is also clear that citizens should be property-owners, in so far as the farmers are obliged to be slaves or serfs of an alien race.

Neither farmers nor artisans should have access to the priesthood. Priestly offices should be confined to the citizens, when age has obliged them to give up their military and political duties, as it is proper for such people to spend their retirement in the service of the gods.

Of course farmers, craftsmen and the labouring class as a whole are necessary adjuncts of a state, but the proper parts of a state are the military and governing sections, these two being, in one sense, permanently, in another sense, temporarily, distinguished.

[8] 1324 b 5–10.          [9] 1328 b 33–1330 a 32.

That Aristotle has Crete in mind, in outlining these provisions, is then made clear by his observation that it is no recent discovery of political philosophers that the state should be segregated into castes and that the military class should be distinguished from the farmers. In fact, he adds, this state of affairs exists even now in Egypt and in Crete, where it is said to have been established in the one case by Sesostris, in the other by Minos. *Syssitia* ('common meals') too are, in his opinion, desirable institutions of well-ordered states, with their costs to be defrayed from part of the revenues of the public lands; and they too have an early history, going back to the time of Minos in Crete, and in Italy being of even earlier origin.

Ideally those who till the soil should be slaves, but not all of the same race and not people of high spirit, so as to ensure that they are well adapted to labour and safe from the possibility of revolution. The next best thing is that they should be foreign serfs of a similar kind of temperament. Those privately employed should be included among the private possessions of the owners of the estates, those who work on the common land should be common property.

Aristotle's reference to the recent invasion of warfare from abroad, at some time in the middle of the fourth century B.C., marks the end of the relative isolation of Crete from the main stream of historical development in the Aegean. From this time on, the island was drawn more and more into contact with the overseas powers of Europe, Asia and Africa. Some of the important consequences of this changed situation of the Hellenistic period will be discussed in later chapters. For the present it will suffice to draw attention to the critical remarks of the historian Polybios about Crete and the Cretans as compared with the general approval expressed by the earlier writers of the fourth century B.C.

For Polybios,[10] writing in the second century B.C., is surprised that the most learned of the ancient writers, including Ephoros, Xenophon, Kallisthenes and Plato, could agree that Crete was both praiseworthy and no different from Sparta, which is for him distinguished by three principal features. By its laws of land tenure all citizens must have equal shares in the public land, no one citizen owning more than another. Secondly, since the

[10] 6.45.1–47.6.

Spartans consider money to be of no value, there is complete absence of jealous rivalry caused by the unequal possession of more or less. Finally, of its officials responsible for the conduct of public affairs, the kings have hereditary office and the Senators tenure for life. In marked contrast, the laws of the Cretans permit the acquisition of an unlimited amount of land. They hold money in such high regard that no gain of any sort is considered disgraceful. Moreover, their system of annual magistracies is of a republican character. It is difficult to understand why earlier writers considered Sparta and Crete so alike. For the Spartans are remarkable in the conduct of internal policy and in their unity. The Cretans, however, are constantly involved in public and private feuds, murders and internal wars.

The literary evidence summarized above, most of it from the fourth century B.C., has to be compared with the evidence now available from inscriptions.[11]

Both Ephoros and Aristotle tells us that there were ten *kosmoi* in the Cretan cities. But the inscriptions do not confirm this statement. In fact, with the exception of one inscription from Hierapytna, and perhaps also one from Gortyn, of the second century B.C., there are no inscriptions which give a list of ten *kosmoi*. Whenever *kosmoi* are enumerated, there are usually fewer than ten. But since we have no inscriptional evidence from the fourth century B.C., we cannot actually say that the evidence of Ephoros and Aristotle is disproved for their time. Nevertheless, it may well be that the information available to Ephoros and Aristotle was either inaccurate or partial in the sense that it was based upon the practice in a few cities or even that ten represented a maximum in certain cities. It does seem very unlikely that there could ever have been ten *kosmoi* in all cities at any one time. It is more likely that the number varied according to the size of the city. For example, in the small backward community of Arcadia in central Crete, two *kosmoi* are recorded at one time in the fifth century B.C. Other inscriptions show that it later became customary to elect three. In such places, the work of administration could have been done by a few supreme magistrates.

The earliest inscriptions from Gortyn (from about 650 to 500 B.C.) make it clear that the personal responsiblity of state

[11] Detailed evidence in Willetts, ASAC 103–51.

officials for state actions has become regular practice. The state is thus now personally identified with the aristocracy. One early Gortynian inscription, for instance, indicates that if a prescribed fine was not paid, the *kosmos* who had been concerned in the affair was under an obligation to pay it himself after he had laid down his office.

It is also made clear that a *kosmos* could not be elected to the same office for a period of three years after he had finished his term. Different intervals were also prescribed for other officials. A legal inscription from Dreros, of approximately the same early date as the Gortynian, forbids the same man to be *kosmos* within a period of ten years; and heavy penalties are prescribed for infringement. It is likely that other cities followed the same practice, with different intervals prescribed between successive tenures of office. This practice was no doubt adopted because it was necessary to terminate, for a definite period, the immunity against civil actions which was a right of *kosmoi* during their term of office. Until this immunity was removed, the *kosmos* could not be obliged to account for his administrative actions and to pay any financial obligation incurred during his term of office.

The Gortynian evidence from the fifth century B.C. certainly makes it clear not only that *kosmoi* could not be involved in litigation whilst they were still holding office but that this temporary immunity was offset by further safeguards against possible abuses. It was illegal, for example, for a runaway serf to be sold within a year if he had taken refuge in a temple, and moreover, if he belonged to a *kosmos,* he could not be sold until his master gave up his office and a year had passed after he had taken refuge. The master was thus prevented from exploiting the advantages of his office, either in the sale of the serf, or in any legal action arising from the transaction.

These legal provisions, laid down in the early fifth century B.C., are consistent with the provision of the Gortyn Code concerning the general immunity of *kosmoi* from litigation during their term of office. Again, if *kosmoi* were convicted in the proceedings which had to take place once they retired from office, they became liable to a fine which might be substantial. For this fine was cumulative from the time an offence was committed, and not merely from the time a *kosmos* retired from office.

A treaty made between Gortyn and Hierapytna with Priansos,

at the beginning of the second century B.C., throws an interesting light upon the formalities of magisterial office. For it appears that magistrates, particularly *kosmoi*, had to wear ceremonial clothes when visiting another city. In a treaty between Hierapytna and Priansos of the same century, the *kosmoi* of one city were allowed entry to the town-hall and also seats in the Assembly of the other city. Envoys of each town were to be properly received by the *kosmoi* of the other, who had to provide them with necessities during their stay or pay them ten staters. Terms of the alliance were to be recited publicly at a festival every year by the *kosmoi*; and ten days' notice of this procedure was to be given by one city to the other. If this obligation was not fulfilled, the *kosmoi* of the offending state were obliged to pay a fine of a hundred staters to the other state. Trespasses against the treaty by magistrates as well as citizens were to be heard before a common tribunal arranged by the *kosmoi*. The *kosmoi* were responsible for publishing the terms of the treaty in the temples of Athene Polias in Hierapytna and Priansos. If the *kosmoi* of one city neglected to carry out certain provisions of the treaty, they incurred a fine of fifty staters each, payable to the other city. Similarly, in a treaty of the same period between Gortyn and Sybrita, if the *kosmoi* failed to publish properly the terms of the treaty, they had to pay a fine to the other city. The element of personal responsibility in matters of state was thus continued into Hellenistic times.

Similarly, the traditions of tribal kinship within the structure of the state also continued into Hellenistic times. We shall have to return to this important aspect of social life in another connexion, but in the meantime it can be briefly illustrated from a treaty between Hierapytna and Praisos of the third century B.C. It was agreed by these two states that a citizen of one of them could assume the full rights of a citizen of the other under certain conditions. Such a person had formally to dispose of his property in his city of origin and likewise renounce his citizenship. The sovereign Assembly of the other city had to decide upon his application by vote. If three votes were cast in opposition, the applicant was not eligible for the grant of citizenship. It is made clear in the agreement that tribal kinship had to be a prior condition of any such transfer of the rights of citizenship. In any case such rights of transfer were individually applied for, considered and conferred. There was no question, here, of automatic reciprocity of civic rights guaranteed by treaty (*isopoliteia*). This practice of *isopoliteia* between Cretan states is, however, well documented, especially in the second century B.C.

We have seen that Aristotle considered that the Assembly in the cities of Crete had no powers except to confirm by vote resolutions previously decided upon by Elders and *kosmoi*. There are no inscriptions of the fourth century B.C. to prove that he was underestimating its powers. But there is some evidence from an earlier date, and even more evidence from later times, to indicate that his statement cannot be accepted as a general truth.

The city of Dreros had one of the earliest known temples to survive from the Iron Age in the whole of Greece. An archaic inscription (belonging to the period between 650 and 500 B.C.) is a further valuable indication of the early development of city-state institutions at Dreros. It is this inscription which forbids the same person to be *kosmos* within a period of ten years. It begins with a formula which shows that it was a decree of the citizens of Dreros meeting in the Assembly. Though it does not tell us who was responsible for the motion, we are not entitled to assume that this responsibility lay with the Council, or the *kosmoi*, or with both combined. It can be more reasonably inferred that the Assembly was responsible for the decree. For the object of the decree was presumably to curtail the privileges of the *kosmoi* and so obstruct any tendency to tyrannical rule. Such being the case, an Assembly of citizens, even though it was a restricted body of aristocratic landlords, would have had a vested interest in this kind of legislation. Whereas the Council, consisting of former *kosmoi*, would not have had such a strong motive.

In the last section of the inscription, three sets of officials, including the *kosmoi*, were bound by oath to observe the enactment. Though we do not know whom the other sets of officials represented, it is logical to assume that one set was appointed by the Council, the other by the Assembly. Thus all three major components of the constitution, *kosmoi*, Council and Assembly, would have been publicly bound by oath to abide by the terms of the legislation.

It appears then that the Assembly, at least in Dreros, at one time had more than merely formal rights of ratification. Furthermore, the formula which introduces the decree is used elsewhere, for example at Gortyn in the third century B.C., when the Assembly of that city passed a famous law authorizing the use of bronze money.

The early Drerian law shows that the development of aristocratic rule was accompanied by sharp internal struggles. Both Council and Assembly derived their powers from tribal forms of social organization, before the rise of the state. Aristotle correctly equated the Cretan Council with the Spartan Elders. For they were originally the elders who formed the tribal council. Similarly, the Assembly of the city-state derived from the old tribal assembly. When the city-states began to develop their typical institutions, the Council and Assembly would still have been close to their tribal origins. But the new, dynamic element in the aristocracies was the *kosmos*, successor to the tribal monarchies. The *kosmoi*, as their name implies, brought order into the new city-states. The Drerian decree gives us an insight into the kind of political conflict which probably occurred in many another state in the course of what must have been a protracted and uneven process.

Evidence about the Council at any period is slight and it is not possible to describe its evolution in any detail. Of the *kosmoi*, however, we can confidently assert that their recruitment remained narrowly based upon a few powerful clan-groupings. Inscriptions of the Hellenistic period prove that close relatives served as magistrates together. It is even likely that secretaries could be selected from the family in power. Nor is it surprising that the Romans, already skilled in the diplomacy of attaching foreign ruling classes to the cause of Roman imperialism, should have allowed the *kosmoi* to continue their rule in the Cretan cities, once they had taken the island by force of arms. Vigorous democracies would have been suppressed. Privileged oligarchies could be tolerated if they remained amenable.

Politically, as well as economically, Crete was a centre of aristocractic rule from the earliest historical period until Roman times. However, the close oligarchy of the early period seems to have been modified to some extent. At least this was the case in a number of city-states where the general citizen body, as we can see from epigraphic references to the role of the Assembly, was increasingly drawn into the legislative and executive apparatus of the state. An increased complexity of constitutional procedure was accompanied by a definite revival, in some places, of the power of the Assembly in the course of the Hellenistic period. This revival points to a greater share of political powers among wider sections of the community of the free citizen class as a whole.

A few documents have fortunately survived to illustrate the factional struggles for power which Aristotle took to be a constant feature of the internal history of the Cretan city-states.

In a decree from Itanos, in East Crete, of the third century B.C., all the citizens were put under an obligation to take an oath of loyalty. *Kosmoi* and priests were made jointly responsible for administering the oath. The *kosmoi* also had to ensure that the oath was taken by anyone arriving in the city after the general ceremony of oath-taking, within a period of ten days. A register of names had to be kept. Negligence on the part of officials was punishable by fines. Anyone refusing the oath was deprived of citizen status. The oath referred to in this decree is apparently that which exists in another contemporary inscription from the city. The city's gods were invoked and the citizen swore not to betray the city or its islands; not to bring enemies in; not to betray the city's ships, its citizens or their property; not to provoke or join an assembly or conspiracy against the city or its people, but to report such matters to the *kosmoi*; to initiate no redistribution of the land, dwellings or dwelling-sites and no cancellation of debts. He was pledged to look to the best interests of his city, observe the laws in force and such as might in future be enacted, and not to desert his city in peace or war.

The likely background to these measures is that the narrow dominant oligarchy had been obliged, under pressure, to enlarge the citizen body. At the same time, by means of these concessions, the basic features of the constitution could be maintained and the enlarged citizen body bound by oath to oppose more radical demands for division of land and property and abolition of debts. It appears that incipient subversion was quelled by widening the constitutional basis of aristocratic rule.

Another important social document, of the late third or early second century B.C., comes from the city of Dreros. This is the inscription which contains the famous oath of the Drerian youth. It illustrates a tendency, which is also apparent in documents

3. Gortyn (from the Acropolis).

4. Section of the Gortyn Code.

5. Phaistos.

from other city-states in this period, for the senior officials to assume firm control of the training of the youth and likewise to ensure that this training was based upon loyalty to existing institutions.

Nevertheless, the Drerian inscription shows that these traditional institutions were being shaken by intense domestic faction as well as by external conflict. Even though we may not be able to postulate a fundamental change in the aristocratic constitution, it is likely that some shift in the balance of power of rival factions preceded the promulgation of this document. Bitter sentiments were expressed towards the city of Lyttos; and the internal situation of Dreros appears to have been highly unstable.

The young men of Dreros, at the annual ceremony of graduation into citizenship, were obliged to swear allegiance to their own city, to its ally, Knossos, and enmity to Lyttos. Treason, factional activity and conspiracy must be formally repudiated; any attempt at such activities must be denounced; and measures were adopted to ensure the annual renewal of the oath. Since denunciation of any conspiratorial activity had to be made before a majority of the *kosmoi*, the assumption is that some of them could not be trusted. The responsibility for taking action against the *kosmoi*, if they were negligent about the oath-taking, was placed upon those who took the oath. No excuse of insolvency was accepted from those who did not pay fines imposed in consequence of such action. Fines were to be shared among members of the *hetaireiai*, as the Cretans called the phratries, either in the city or on garrison duty. Though *kosmoi* had to officiate at the ceremony of oath-taking, they were under the supervision of the Council and subject to the vigilance of the young men just admitted to citizenship. If Councillors were negligent in their duties, they were obliged to pay a double fine. This double fine had to be exacted by the collectors of public funds and shared among members of the *hetaireiai*. The whole citizen population was thus alerted to ensure the imposition of the oath of allegiance upon the youth who were immediately themselves obliged to assume an attitude of vigilance towards senior officials.

We can therefore conclude that, at least in some cities, there were intense internal struggles in the Hellenistic period, associated with the efforts of the rank and file citizens to advance their own political power at the expense of the old-established narrow oligarchy. More radical demands for re-division of land and abolition of debts probably met, at best, with only a limited success, although, in the absence of direct evidence, it is impossible to admit even this cautious possibility with any certainty. For there is no indication that such demands were ever associated with a movement for the emancipation of the serfs, the majority of the population of the city-states, even when these states were at war with one another. Though the states were often in violent collision, their ruling classes were at least united by one overriding bond of self-interest, the need to maintain the subjection of the peasantry. This continual subjection was essential to the functioning of Cretan aristocracy.

In other respects, disunity among the governing classes was becoming more marked, internally and externally. The Itanian oath exemplifies the internal disunity. The Drerian oath relates internal disunity to an external enemy. A revolution in Gortyn, at the end of the third century B.C., dramatically typifies the main features of the chronic political impasse which had overtaken the aristocracies and which foreign conquest was eventually to resolve. This revolution took the form of conflict between young and old citizens, a conflict which Plato as well as Aristotle had foreseen as a possibility and which the traditional educational system was designed to prevent.

In his discussion of the events of the period 221–219 B.C., Polybios tells us[12] how disaster overtook the Lyttians. The Knossians, in alliance with the Gortynians, had been able to control the whole of Crete, except for Lyttos, which firmly resisted subjection. War was therefore begun against Lyttos, the intention being to destroy the city so as to offer a grim warning to the rest of Crete. However, the unity of the opposition could not be maintained and a group of cities deserted the alliance and joined with Lyttos.

Civil war now broke out in Gortyn. The older citizens sided with Knossos, the younger with Lyttos. Though surprised by these events, Knossos was able to enlist the help of a force of Aetolians. The Gortynian party which favoured them then seized the citadel, the Knossians and their Aetolian supporters were allowed to enter the city, and the young Gortynian rebels were exiled or killed. Those who were exiled held the harbour

[12] 4.53.3–55.6.

of Gortyn and seized the harbour of neighbouring Phaistos. From these vantage points they maintained their armed struggle against their opponents in the city. They were able to continue their resistance as a result of the intervention of King Philip of Macedon, after Lyttos had been destroyed and its women and children carried off to Knossos.

Documents of the Hellenistic period then, and from Itanos, Dreros and Gortyn in particular, confirm in detail the warnings of the philosophers about the dangers of breakdown in a system which they admired despite defects they were obliged to recognize. The earlier epigraphic documents, however, only tell us, though often in a fragmentary way, how the aristocratic apparatus of government had been built up. To this aspect of the development of the bureaucratic administration we must now turn.

As we have seen, the earliest inscriptions from Gortyn reveal that the personal responsibility of state officials for their activities on behalf of the state, a general feature of government in Greek antiquity, was already well established in the Cretan aristocractic city-states by the sixth century B.C. By the early part of the following century divisions of administrative function become apparent in the Gortynian evidence. For example, the *ksenios kosmos* ('aliens' magistrate') was a principal official whose duties lay with foreigners, such as resident aliens, and others, such as freedmen, who were not included among the tribal organizations of the free citizenry. A secretary, or recorder, to the *ksenios kosmos* is mentioned in the Gortyn Code. One of the *kosmoi*, certainly in Gortyn by the Hellenistic period, received the title of *hiarorgos* ('sacral'). We can assume that he had a special responsibility for religious affairs. The judicial functions of the *kosmoi* and of the specialist judges called *dikastai* will be mentioned later.

In addition to specialist *kosmoi* and judges, there were other officials with particular duties to perform. The *titai* ('public indemnifiers'), as we know from Gortyn, existed from the period of the earliest written evidence. Though we cannot be quite certain about their role, it is clear that they could exercise supervisory duties over the *kosmoi*, from whom they could exact fines. Their functions were probably similar to those of the *logistai* who are mentioned in the decree of the city of Itanos of the third century B.C., which obliged the citizens to take the oath discussed above. If they were negligent in carrying out the provisions of the decree, each of the *kosmoi* had to pay a fine of a hundred drachmas to the state. The fines might be presented to the *logistai* ('commissioners'), but the *praktores* ('bailiffs'), who exacted the fines, had to hand them over to the incoming *kosmos*. The *logistai* are mentioned in Crete only in this one document. In Athens and in other places, however, we know they were in charge of public administration. The Athenian *logistai* were a board of ten persons who were chosen by lot from members of the Council. Magistrates had to submit accounts to them when they retired from office. Since their duties were similar, the *titai* of Gortyn could also have been appointed by the Council, with a particular responsibility for looking after the payment of fines. There is some evidence to suggest that if the *titai* were negligent in exacting fines from *kosmoi* after they had become liable, they were punished by having to pay twice the amount themselves.

Special mention deserves to be made of some of the other officials who are named in various documents. The *karpodaistai* ('produce-dividers') occur in a very interesting inscription from Gortyn of the early fifth century B.C. They appear to have had the task of collecting produce for the upkeep of *syssitia* ('common meals'). If such be the case, the Gortynian state had already taken over responsibility for collecting duly assessed amounts of produce from its citizens for the *syssitia*, as a kind of recognized tribute. *Agoranomoi* ('market-supervisors') are also mentioned at Gortyn, but not before the first century B.C. However, it is fairly certain that officials of this kind did exist at an earlier date and in other cities. There were usually three of them at Gortyn, and they had the assistance of a secretary.

The *agora* or market-place of the city was a recognized place of assembly. The *prytaneion* or town-hall was just as important in the civic life of the community and it is frequently mentioned in Cretan inscriptions. Another chief centre of activity for the citizens was the gymnasium, the Cretan term for which was *dromos* ('a running-track' or 'sports ground').

The *chreophylakion* (which was not an exclusively Cretan institution) was an office in which the register of public debtors was kept. It is mentioned in a number of Cretan cities, Knossos,

Lato and Olous, Gortyn and Polyrhenia, in the course of the second century B.C. This evidence suggests that the *chreophylakion* was now playing an important role in the diplomacy of city-states and in their financial transactions. For example, in one of the Cretan inscriptions, the cities of Lato and Olous agreed to submit the arbitration of a dispute to a third party, Knossos. They were pledged to abide by a decision. Moreover, as a symbol of good faith, they were bound by a sum of money, payable to Knossos, and had to provide, within a stipulated period, sureties at Knossos in guarantee of the payment of the sum of money. The sureties were to be provided through the medium of the *chreophylakoin* at Knossos. In other words, Lato and Olous were to purchase credits on persons at Knossos and deposit the titles with the *chreophylakion* at Knossos or purchase credits of which titles were already deposited.

Thus the *chreophylakion* was a useful medium in commercial transactions of credit. But, if the arrangement made by the Knossians was not abnormal, the method worked to the distinct advantage of the creditor. For, if the treaty were violated, the Knossian magistrates had merely to take action against their own citizens because the treaty allowed Knossos to choose Knossian sureties. Thereby the Knossians enjoyed initial ample protection. Moreover, if one of the two contracting cities failed to abide by the terms of agreement, the other city could count on compensation in full.

The official court of justice, known as the *dikasterion*, is mentioned in the Gortyn Code. Its role in the life of the city-state will be the theme of the following chapter.

# V

◇◇◇◇◇◇◇◇◇◇◇◇◇◇◇◇◇◇◇◇◇◇◇◇◇◇◇◇◇◇◇◇

# Law and Legal Procedure

◇◇◇◇◇◇◇◇◇◇◇◇◇◇◇◇◇◇◇◇◇◇◇◇◇◇◇◇◇◇◇◇

T H E aristocratic states thus developed forms of public power primarily to consolidate the rule of a privileged citizenry over the non-citizen members of the community, and especially the peasant serfs. There was another purpose also in this promotion of officialdom. The authority of the elders of the clans, from whom higher officials were recruited, had to be supported, through the fabric of the growing state apparatus, by the armed citizen youth. This military body defended the state against external enemies. Internally it constituted a kind of permanent police force, personifying the power of the state.

This power began to be expressed in legal sanctions, as tribal custom yielded to written law. The alphabet had arrived in Greece along the trade routes. An increasing command of writing accompanied increased commercial enterprise. Written laws are among the major expressions of the maturing aristocratic state in Crete. They are at once a symbol and a record of the authority of the new order.

We saw from a number of examples in the preceding chapter how the laws had acquired, from the standpoint of officialdom, a sacrosanct character in the preservation of constitutions. All this was quite consistent with the role of the law in the establishment of early constitutions and particularly in the promulgation of the sanctions which governed the periods of tenure of the chief magistrates. Thus it may perhaps be inferred from the earliest complete Cretan law from Dreros, which limited the tenure of the *kosmos* to ten years, that another Drerian clan was to have the exclusive right of tenure for the same period. In contemporary Gortyn, we have seen that the magisterial terms of office were also the subject of legal enactment.

There is little doubt that, when the *kosmoi* took over the leadership of the community from the tribal monarchies, they carried out judicial duties, in the same way as they had usurped the military functions of the kings. This development can be illustrated from the evidence of the earliest Gortynian inscriptions. As time went on, their legal functions became more general and supervisory. Thus the Council, composed of ex-*kosmoi*, is shown by the epigraphic evidence from several cities to act as a guardian body of the laws of the state. In the Gortyn Code, the *kosmoi* can act as a judicial authority only in the case where the marriage of an heiress comes into conflict with the normally sanctioned procedure. Even so, the *ksenios kosmos* was still, as we see from the Code, a specialist official with important duties connected with persons outside the tribal grouping of the citizen body, such as foreigners and freedmen. Similarly, in the sphere of religion, the *kosmos hiarorgos* still maintained his specialist role in the inscriptions of Hellenistic times.

But the simultaneous increase of the political duties of the *kosmoi* and the increasing complexity of legal procedure made necessary the appearance of special officials called *dikastai* ('judges'). Moreover, the powers of the state had so far expanded that these *dikastai* were assigned to different spheres of duty as a result of the ensuing volume and variety of litigation. Some *dikastai* had to deal with cases involving inheritances, others with pledges. Still others, judges of the *hetaireiai* as they were called, perhaps had to deal with matters of tribal law and custom, adapting them to the new requirements of the state. The judges had public officials assigned to their courts who maintained records and also assisted in procedural matters.

The Gortyn Code tells us a good deal about the way in which the judges did their work, though it is not clear how they were appointed or paid. In the Code, each case was tried before a single judge, who heard the whole of it. There is no indication of trial by jury. Sometimes, however, the judge was required to 'give judgement', sometimes to 'decide on oath'. As the Code itself announces: 'Whatever is written for the judge to decide according to witnesses or by oath of denial, he shall decide as is written, but in other matters he shall decide under oath accord-to the pleas.'[1] These witnesses, however, were not witnesses to facts, but to the proper performance of processual acts. It was not their business to adduce evidence in settlement of disputed facts.

That is how the procedure was interpreted by J. W. Headlam.[2] The interpretation corresponds with other early evidence, establishing a marked distinction between the witness in our sense, whose function is to clarify a matter in dispute, and the earlier use, prior to written records and written contracts, of witnesses as absolute proofs of facts.

When the pleas of both sides of a case under trial had been heard, the judge usually then took an oath and made his decision. But in some cases it was ordained that this decision should not be made by argument before a sworn judge but by the solemn oath of the accused persons. When witnesses had testified and pleas had been established, but there still remained a point of fact to be settled, the law sometimes prescribed that the judge pass judgement immediately, instead of judging upon oath. In such cases, the defendants had to clear themselves by oath or pay the prescribed penalty, and, since the judge did not have to exercise his discretion, he was not obliged to make his judge-ment under oath. But where the decision involved matters of right not decided by law, or on the amount of a penalty not prescribed by the law, or on some factual matter which had not been settled by witnesses or the purgatory oath of the defendant, the judge had to make his judgement upon oath. Since he was judging on the basis of his personal opinions, the oath was a public manifestation of his honest conduct.

By the beginning of the fifth century B.C., then, the judge had become an important official with responsible and detailed func-tions. Later, as the idea of law assumed an increasingly abstract, absolutist authority, the jurisdiction of specialist judges could sometimes be extended beyond their own city-state frontiers. The extent of this practice is documented by inscriptions in the two or three centuries which preceded the Christian era. It

---

[1] *Leg.Gort.* XI.26ff. cf. Diamond, PL 366.          [2] Headlam, PGI.

became common for a Greek city to loan judges to other cities, sometimes to deal with cases which had multiplied beyond the capacities of the local authorities because of war or internal conflict, sometimes to act as impartial arbitrators in matters which seemed to require extraordinary measures. Such judges would be nominated by special decree after their services had been formally petitioned by the city which needed them. The judges and their secretaries acted as official representatives and were treated like ambassadors. When their work was done, they received public eulogies and other honours.

This interesting practice can be illustrated for Crete by a decree of the city of Malla, in the latter part of the second century B.C. The highest honours are awarded to judges from Knossos and Lyttos, as saviours, defenders and champions. We gather from the decree that Malla had fallen into a state of extreme disorder and confusion. Rights of property and rules of contract had ceased to be respected or upheld. An appeal was therefore made to the neighbouring cities of Knossos and Lyttos who despatched respectively one and two judges. We must suppose from the record that their work was conspicuously successful.

Historically, the state is a man-made institution. In Greece, its growth was accompanied by the subordination of other social classes to the citizen community and by the curtailment of the rights of women as compared with men. Thus, for example, in what is probably a late passage of the Gortyn Code, mention is made of yet another special category of judges, 'orphan-judges' —perhaps a fairly recent innovation—who were involved in a process of extending the power of the state to promote the property rights of men at the expense of women. For the 'orphan-judges' were officials appointed to supervise the affairs of orphans or minors. The appointment of such officials, taken in conjunction with amendments in the regulations for administration of estates of heiresses, involved a curtailment of the customary rights of kinsfolk and especially of kinsfolk in the female line.[3]

The range of topics covered by the surviving legal inscriptions of the early historical period further illustrates the consequences of the growth of private property and of the family at the

[3] *Leg.Gort.* XII. 6–17; Willetts, ASAC 78–80, 206.

expense of communal rights and old tribal custom. Aside from the regulations of the Gortyn Code, we have examples of public legislation concerned with such matters as water supplies, funerals, damages, securities, mortgages, arbitration and public health.[4]

For example, at Gortyn the supply of river-water was already the subject of legislation in the earlier part of the fifth century B.C. In one inscription from this period, the right of citizens to divert the river-water to irrigate their own land is recognized, but subject to the proviso that the level of the water should not fall below a definite limit at the bridge in the market-place. Laws of this kind were probably common in most Greek city-states from early times, as is confirmed by some remarks in Plato's *Laws*: 'And so far as water-supplies are concerned too, there are excellent old laws laid down for farmers which we need not draw upon in our inquiry. Suffice to say that he who wants to bring water to his own land can do so, beginning with the public streams, but without undercutting the open wells of any private person. He can divert it how he likes, except through a house or temples and tombs and without doing any damage apart from the actual digging of the channel. . . . And if, when rain comes, a farmer on lower ground does any damage to the farmer on land above or adjoining his own by preventing its outflow, or, conversely, if the farmer on higher ground damages the farmer on land below by rashly releasing the flood-water, and if, in consequence, they be unwilling to come to some agreement among themselves in the matter, anyone who likes can call in a city-steward in the city or a land-steward in the country so as to get a definite order as to what each is to do. The one who fails to comply with the order is liable to be charged with ill-will and malice, and, on conviction, to have to pay double the damage to the injured party for refusing to obey the authorities.'[5]

Other pieces of legislation from Gortyn in the early part of the fifth century B.C. have a similar purport to the latter part of Plato's suggested regulation. One such law sought to prevent water being used so carelessly as to damage a neighbour's land and laid down a daily penalty to be claimed from the person responsible. On the other hand, another law provided that, if a farmer brought water over a neighbour's land after due notice,

[4] Willetts, ASAC 214–17.                    [5] Pl.*Lg*. 844 a–d.

he was not liable to any penalty, even if the water failed to drain away. But if the water had been brought over the land without authority, then the person responsible could be fined.

Early Gortynian legislation concerning funerals is again by no means unique. We know that such early laws existed elsewhere, including Athens, Sparta and Syracuse. These laws have one thing in common—they were directed against the participation of women. The state authorities were legislating on behalf of the patriarchal family and against the wider circle of the tribal kinsfolk, especially the female kin and their unrestrained public demonstrations of mourning. The same trend of seeking to restrict responsibility for funeral ceremonies to the relatives of the deceased is apparent in a number of inscriptions from Gortyn.

Again Plato's *Laws* can be called upon to witness the traditional nature of this trend:[6] 'The laying out of the corpse and suchlike are to be done in accordance with the custom governing such matters, but custom has to give way to regulations of state law of the following sort: To enjoin or prohibit weeping for the dead is unseemly, but wailing and loud lamentation outside the house should be forbidden, the carrying out of the corpse into the open roadway and crying aloud while it is borne through the streets prevented, and the mourners are to be outside the city before day dawns.'

It is not surprising, in conditions where private property was being developed, that security, mortage, damages, arbitration and such-like were matters to which the legislators gave early and systematic attention. Some interesting examples of these types of legislation have survived, chiefly from Gortyn, in the provisions of the so-called Second Code, of about the same date as the Great Code, only a part of a few columns of which have, however, survived: and also from Knossos.[7]

The Gortynian legislation under this head, for instance, granted the right to the owner to exchange an injured animal with an animal belonging to someone else which did the damage. Failure to comply obliged the owner of the animal which did the damage to pay the simple value. (It can be assumed that the animals in question were oxen.) When a pig wounded or killed an ox, the pig became the property of the owner of the ox.

[6] *Ibid.*, 959 e–960 a.        [7] Willetts, ASAC 217–21.

Similar penalties applied in case of injury to horses, mules and asses. Detailed procedures were laid down in case the injured beast was dead or it was otherwise not possible to show the damage to the other party in the case.

If persons who received birds or beasts deposited in trust for use or for other purposes did not restore them at the due time, they became liable to pay the simple value. However, if anyone holding such property in trust denied his responsibility and he was adjudged guilty at law he was then liable to pay double the value and a fine to the state as well. The fine to the state was presumably imposed because of the trouble caused in the legal process and perhaps also because a denial of the responsibility caused offence to the state. The amount of the fine to be paid is not specified. We must assume that it was either a fixed sum or an assessment based on the value of the damage paid privately.

There is some fragmentary legal evidence from Knossos to show that similar regulations existed there as at Gortyn concerning damages. Thus, anyone responsible for breaking the horns of an animal had to pay the owner a fine. The purchaser of an animal was allowed five days to return it if he so decided. But he had to pay a daily indemnity for loss of working value, unless the animal was not broken into work.

There also survive pieces of legislation from the early fifth century B.C. at Gortyn about the intervals laid down as a matter of procedure before judgement was delivered in certain cases. In a dispute about boundaries, for example, fifteen days' delay was granted, probably to allow the grounds of dispute to be investigated. However, if the prescribed period of delay was exceeded, the judge himself became as much liable as if he had refused to undertake the legal process, unless some reasonable excuse could be offered. But judges of the *hetaireia* or those concerned with securities were obliged to give judgement on the same day as the parties to a dispute presented themselves, or at latest on the day following.

Another rather later law from Gortyn is the only legal evidence from that city for the existence of arrangements for private arbitration, which could be requested by either or both parties to a dispute.

Other Gortynian legislation of the early fifth century B.C. was concerned with the illegal seizure, in the form of securities, of persons, crops, clothing and ornaments. In the same inscription which provides this evidence, there is mention of lands, the property of the state, leased for cultivation, of which the sale or mortgage was declared illegal.

Another fragment deals with the illegal seizure of trees, houses and possessions not belonging to a debtor. Some items of personal property of a free man could not be seized as securities. Those specified included his arms (a prohibition common to most similar Greek legislation), loom, wool, iron tools, ox-yoke, plough, hand-mill stones, marriage bed, certain other utensils, and perhaps also clothes and ornaments. In the same text there is a provision allowing a man handicapped by old age or by other reasons to appoint a deputy to make a seizure of securities on his account.

The Gortyn Code itself gives us much more detailed information about the laws of property brought into being by the social changes of the early historical period. Much of this information will be drawn upon to substantiate the arguments of following chapters. The Code gives us a valuable insight into the early phases of the emergence of the abstract powers of law operating on behalf of the state, as well as the status and responsibilities of the state functionaries operating in the sphere of law to promote the growth of state institutions, of property and the family. Although the evidence relating to the growth of similar institutions elsewhere in ancient Greece is but partial, we have enough information concerning the laws of inheritance in general to justify a comparison with Athens and Sparta. Judged from this perspective, the Gortyn Code is the product of a social system economically more backward in the early fifth century B.C. than Athens had been in the sixth, but at the same time more advanced than Sparta was in the fourth.

The style in which the Code is written expresses a distinct secular outlook. Regulations are couched uniformly as conditional sentences in the third person. The assumed facts are stated, the legal consequences or provisions follow, normally expressed in the equivalent of a future tense or imperative mood. As in other early Codes, such as the Code of Hammurabi, there is no command or prohibition in the second person or formulation of rules as divine sanctions. A. S. Diamond has categorized this body of Gortynian law as a dividing line between the end of primitive law and the beginning of mature law, this beginning being especially emphasized by the increase in its procedural technicalities. As he put it, the devolution of judicial functions upon officers of justice must be added to the increase in populations, the growth of commerce and the spreading use of writing, in recognizing this significant change. A subordinate judge has no power to depart from the laws which are his instructions. The whole system of judicature, including the rules of law which it applies, becomes an increasingly important and self-contained department of the state. In the enactment of new laws *legal* reasons for their enactment become common and influential. New rules are enacted not simply because they are just, though in the long run that consequence will follow, but to assist in the trial of cases. It is in this context that the analysis of the procedure of the Code by Headlam, discussed above, has a special importance.[8]

The topics covered by the Code are arranged not by reference to legal principles but the need to group together statutes covering like or similar circumstances. Thus there are regulations relating to suits which concerned the ownership of actual or alleged slaves; such matters as rape and adultery; marriage and the rights of property; the division of property among children and heirs; the sale and the mortgaging of the family property; the repayment of ransoms; the children of mixed marriages; the responsibility for the acts of a slave; a most important and highly interesting series of regulations about the marriage of the heiress and the disposal of her property; the procedure for adoption; as well as a variety of provisions in certain special cases.

[8] Diamond, PL 340-9; Headlam, PGI.

# VI

❖❖❖❖❖❖❖❖❖❖❖❖❖❖❖❖❖❖❖❖❖❖❖❖❖❖❖❖❖❖❖❖❖❖❖❖❖

## The Citizens

❖❖❖❖❖❖❖❖❖❖❖❖❖❖❖❖❖❖❖❖❖❖❖❖❖❖❖❖❖❖❖❖❖❖❖❖❖

HAVING examined the political system developed by the Dorian aristocracies of Crete and the legal apparatus which gave it authoritative sanction, we must now turn our attention to the social institutions of the free citizen class. The free citizens, who formed a minority of the population of each city-state, were a ruling class of landlords from which the governing élite was recruited. They were still, however, organized on a tribal basis at the time of the Gortyn Code. This tribal basis had been modified by the growth of the state apparatus, by the development of private property and the rise of the family as an institution. Nevertheless, many of the characteristic features of social life among the citizens were survivals, in some cases very vigorous survivals, from tribal society adapted to the city-state.

The tribe is named in the Gortyn Code and in inscriptions from other cities. So is the clan; and, as we have seen, the *kosmoi* continued to be recruited from ruling clans. Women were still enumerated in the tribes, but the phratry, which was known in Crete as the *hetaireia*, had become an exclusive association of male citizens, denying political rights to women and to all non-citizens. It can be inferred from the Gortyn Code that the *hetaireia* played a part of political importance in the development of the aristocratic system, as that system progressed from a tribal association based on kinship to a firmly-knit privileged

85

corporation based on narrow political rights of citizenship. But evidence from succeeding centuries shows that, in comparison with the corresponding association of the youth, which was still flourishing in Hellenistic times, the *hetaireiai* rapidly began to lose their importance once the central authority of the state was firmly established. For their purpose became more and more restricted to the system of communal meals (the *syssitia*), another principal feature of social life derived from tribalism.

These *syssitia* were characteristic institutions not only of Crete, but of various other parts of ancient Greece, including Sparta. Aristotle expressed his preference for the Cretan system of *syssitia* as compared with the Spartan. 'The Cretan administration of the *syssitia*', he wrote, 'is better than the Spartan. For, while in Sparta each citizen pays a fixed contribution, failing which he is legally deprived of a share in government, in Crete the system is more communal; since, out of all the crops and the cattle produced from the public lands and the tributes paid by the serfs, one part is devoted to the worship of the gods and the upkeep of public services, and the other part to the *syssitia*, so that all the citizens are maintained from common funds, men, women and children.'[1]

The stability of its agrarian system is the key to the enduring character of Cretan aristocratic society. The *syssitia* organization was one of the basic characteristics of the system. Both in Sparta and in Crete this organization became modified to serve as a central part of a patriarchal slave-system whose purpose was to produce direct means of subsistence and to serve as a point of departure for the exacting of tribute by the state, especially as rent in kind began to be supplemented by money-rent. When Aristotle praised the more communal system of the Cretans, with its aim of maintaining all citizens from public resources, he stressed the part played in the contribution to these resources by the regular tributes drawn from the serfs. This information can be supplemented by other evidence from another ancient writer on Cretan history, Dosiadas. He tells how the people of Lyttos pooled their resources for the *syssitia* in this way: 'Every man contributes a tithe of his crops to his *hetaireia*, as well as the income from the state which the magis-

[1] *Pol.* 1272 a.

trates divide among the households of all citizens; and each serf pays one Aiginetan stater per head.'[2]

The right to carry arms continued to be one of the familiar distinctive rights of the Cretan aristocrat. So much so that Aristotle mentions the clever device of the Cretans in conceding to their serfs the same rights as they have themselves except to forbid them gymnastic exercises and the possession of arms.[3] We have seen how, in the Song of Hybrias, the implications of the privilege of bearing arms are elaborated. The master in that poem signifies boastingly that his arms are substitutes for the labourer's tools, signs of his superiority over the labourer as well as the means by which his wealth is gained. This wealth of which Hybrias boasts was landed wealth, and nobility was based on its possession.[4]

The distribution of the land and its servile cultivators among the Dorian tribesmen brought about successive modifications in the system of inheritance among the ruling clans. We saw how the Minoan palace 'households' exercised their influence in the one-sided development of Bronze Age economy. Now, in the new conditions of the Iron Age city-state, the tendency developed for smaller units of relationship to grow within the wider circle of the clan system of the rulers. This tendency was most marked in the basic institution of the *oikos* ('household'), which was closely bound up with the possession of the family estate, called the *klaros* ('lot').

The Gortyn Code provided that the father should have power over the children and the property to divide it among them; that, as long as the parents lived, there was no need for division; and that, if a man or woman died, their children, or grandchildren, or great-grandchildren, should have the property. Therefore the headship of the *oikos* and the ownership of property were vested in the parent as long as he lived and wanted to retain his proprietary right. Even when he was dead, the sons need not necessarily divide the estate among themselves but could operate a joint ownership of the single *oikos* of the dead parent. The eldest would probably, in such cases, take the house, fulfilling his duties to the family altars, duties which now devolved upon him as the head of the family.[5]

In case a man or woman died and left no children, it was

[2] *Ap.* Ath. 143 a–b.   [3] *Pol.* 1264 a 12.   [4] P. 12.   [5] *Leg.Gort.* IV.24ff.

enacted that the deceased's brothers, and brothers' children, or grandchildren, should have the property. If there were none of these, then the *epiballontes*, as the heirs who had the next claim were called, inherited the property.[6] In other words, in the direct line, a man's descendants down to great-grandchildren inherited the estate. But where there was inheritance through a brother, the kinship terminated with the brother's grandchildren, these being great-grandchildren to the nearest common ancestor with the previous owner of the estate. The *epiballontes* were kinsmen in any degree who, though not members of the *oikos*, belonged to the same clan as the members of the *oikos*. Their residual rights dated back to the time when the land and its attached peasants had been divided out in equal lots among the clansmen of the Dorian tribes who had spread over Crete. But as the more narrowly based *oikos* developed within the clan, the ownership of estates became confined to this more restricted circle of kinship. As yet, at the time of the Gortyn Code, there was no trace of free testamentary disposition of property, which was to disrupt the traditional system by the time of Polybios. Landed wealth still maintained its dominant position because wealth in the form of money was still a novelty in comparison. However, the rise of the individual family had begun to be promoted by state legislation on the basis, where necessary and acceptable, of the marriage of kin within the *oikos*, and of division of the inheritance. Thus the *oikos* preserved the collective custom of clan organization, out of which it grew, within its narrower sphere. Nevertheless it was, at the same time, a transitional form of organization, preparing the way for the autonomous family, based upon private property. For the introduction of coined money into Crete at the beginning of the fifth century B.C. gave stimulus to the dissolution of the old collective system and eventually brought about that alienation of estates which had become general by Hellenistic times.

In the light of these developments, the old tribal custom of adoption assumed a new importance and was modified accordingly. When possession of property had been wholly vested in the clan, a dead man's property would have been shared among his clansmen according to their degree of relationship. As the *oikos* developed, the clansmen's rights became more and more

[6] *Ibid.* V.9ff.

formal. Membership of the *oikos* involved such social and religious duties as the upkeep of the estate and the fulfilment of family obligations, particularly those associated with the maintenance of rites at the founder's tomb. These duties were the special responsibility of the heir to the estate. Therefore, until free testamentary disposition became recognized as normal practice, the head of the *oikos* must have had to ensure that he had a suitably responsible successor from within the *oikos*. With the weakening of the old clan ties of kinship and inheritance, it seems that the system of adoption had become, through the apparatus of the *hetaireiai*, a responsibility of the state and no longer a direct concern of the clans.

It was laid down in the Gortyn Code that an adoption might be made without any restriction. The ceremony of adoption was held in the market-place before the assembled citizens and the adopter had to give a sacrificial victim and a quantity of wine to his *hetaireia*.

In the case where there were no legitimate children and the adopted person inherited all the property, he had to carry out all the duties of the adopter in social and religious matters. Where he was not willing to assume such duties, the property was inherited by the *epiballontes*. In the case where there were legitimate children, the adopted person inherited a proportion of the property equal to that which sisters received from their brothers. If the adopted person died without legitimate children, then the property passed to the adopter's *epiballontes*. The adopter was allowed to renounce the adoption if he so wished. A woman could not make an adoption, nor could a person of immature years.

The provision that property had to pass to the *epiballontes* if the adopted son died without legitimate heirs makes clear that the purpose of adoption was to ensure a succession in the male line.[7]

The detailed series of regulations concerning the heiress in the Gortyn Code are of the utmost interest to the social historian. These regulations make clear that the members of her tribe could still claim rights of marriage to an heiress when, in certain circumstances, she did not marry the next of kin. Therefore we must assume that the rule of tribal endogamy was still

[7] *Ibid.* X.34–XI.23.

normally preserved. This means that the *epiballontes* formed an exogamous clan grouping who normally intermarried with what were termed their *kadestai*, forming another exogamous clan grouping. *Epiballontes* and *kadestai* were complementary terms which denoted close mutual ties of obligation established by kinship in the one case and by marriage in the other. The basis of this system was archaic, similar to tribal customs which have been observed by anthropologists in more recent times, depending upon a continuous intermarriage of cross-cousins, the form of marriage relations resulting from the intermarriage in each generation of two exogamous groups, relatives being classified according as they belong to one's own group or to the other. Close ties of obligation, loyalty and respect were thereby established far outside an immediate family circle.

Now the laws of inheritance in Athens became quite firmly based upon the principle of succession in the male line. A daughter could inherit only when she had no brothers, and was regarded as an heiress and therefore a means of transferring property to another male. Unless her father had arranged otherwise, she could, if she was unmarried, be claimed in marriage by the next of kin, who was in a position to marry her by divorcing his own wife. If she was married, her marriage could be terminated and the next of kin could demand to marry her. The property of the heiress passed to her son when he came of age.

The Gortyn Code, however, portrays an earlier state of affairs when there had been less curtailment of the rule of exogamy, according to which husband and wife must come from different clans. Hence the provisions of the Code relating to the heiress have sometimes been looked upon as the product of a more enlightened legislation, with more respect for the rights of women than the Athenian. In contemporary Sparta, however, women were in a more favourable social position even than in Crete. The truth is that the more private property and the family developed at the expense of the old tribal institutions, the more diminished became the rights of women compared with men. This is made quite clear by comparing the position of the Gortynian heiress with that of her Athenian counterpart.

According to the Code, an heiress at Gortyn was a daughter without a father and a brother of the same father. She could inherit her father's property but was obliged to marry the next of kin. Her immediate next of kin was her paternal uncle. If she had several paternal uncles, the oldest of them had the prior claim to marry her. When there were a number of heiresses and paternal uncles, they were under obligation to marry in order of age. When there were no paternal uncles, the heiress had to marry her paternal cousin. When there were several of them, the oldest had the prior claim. When there were several heiresses and paternal cousins, they were under obligation to marry in order of the age of the brothers.

The interests of the individual patriarchal family were thus being promoted by state legislation, which encouraged the marriage of kin within the household as opposed to cross-cousin marriage between clans. But these novel trends were still opposed by other sanctions dependent upon the survival of older matrilineal traditions. The evidence shows that property and land were still to a significant degree in the hands of women.

In the case, for example, where the heiress and the claimant were too young to marry, the heiress was allowed the house, if there was a house, together with half the income from the property, while the claimant next of kin was entitled to the other half. Where the heiress was old enough to marry but there was no male next of kin to claim her in marriage, she was allowed possession of the property and could marry as she pleased within the tribe. If no one from the tribe came forward, she could then accept anyone who was willing to marry her. Where a married woman became an heiress, she was allowed to terminate the marriage if she wished, even against her husband's wishes. In such a case, if there were children of the marriage, she could marry again within the tribe, provided she shared the property with the children. The heiress and her remaining property thus remained within the tribe. Where there were no children, however, the heiress was obliged to marry the next of kin. Both could refuse the obligation by sacrificing half the property. If there was no next of kin, the heiress could then marry within the tribe, or, if no suitor presented himself, outside it. When an heiress became a widow she could, if she had children, marry again within the tribe, but could not be obliged to do so. But if there were no children, she was then obliged to marry the next of kin.[8]

[8] *Ibid.* VII.15–IX.24; XII.6–19; Willetts, ASAC 69–84, CK.

Another remarkable provision of the Code is that marriage could be contracted by a free woman with a serf. If the serf lived with the free woman, the children of the marriage were free. If the woman went to live with the man, however, the children were servile. A woman who married twice could thus have both free and servile children. Since there is no mention of the contingency, we must assume that marriages between free men and serf women were not legally recognized.[9]

Husband and wife were allowed the right of divorce if either wished. The wife was allowed her own property and a sum of money if the husband caused the divorce. We can infer that the wife retained her own property after marriage, though the produce from it was shared with her husband. The inference is confirmed by the procedure prescribed in case of the death of a husband or wife. The property which the wife had received by dowry or inheritance remained in her control; the husband could neither sell it nor mortgage it.

If a free woman had a child after divorce, she was obliged to take the child to her former husband at his house in the presence of witnesses; and if he refused to accept the child, the mother then was entitled to rear or expose it as she wished. If the woman exposed the child before taking it to the former husband's house she was fined.[10]

The regulations laid down about the division of property among the children of the family are of great interest. The father had power over the children and the division of property among them while the mother had power over her own property. Normally, there was no obligation to make a division of the property while the parents were living. If, however, one of the sons was condemned to pay a fine, his due portion might then be given to him.

When the father died, the houses in the town and anything in the houses, provided they were not occupied by a serf belonging to the country estate, together with the sheep and larger animals not belonging to a serf, went to the sons. All the rest of the property was fairly divided, the sons receiving two parts, the daughters one part each. When the mother died, her property was divided in the same way. In cases where there was no property except a house, the daughters had their share as pre-

[9] *Leg.Gort.* VII.1–10.     [10] *Ibid.* II.45–IV.14.

scribed. Houses in the town are given special consideration because the town was the centre of the social life of the citizen class.

If a father wanted to make a gift to his daughter on her marriage, he could do so within prescribed limits. While the parents remained alive, there was a safeguard against a division of the estate. Elsewhere it is clear that the law worked in favour of such a division if the heirs were in agreement. It is likely that the impulse towards division of the estates was prompted by the growth of a money economy and therefore of individual as opposed to collective tenure.

Houses occupied by serfs belonged, liked the serfs themselves, to the estate and so were treated as income-producing property, in which the daughters shared. The sons, however, were given clear preference over the daughters in the division of the inheritance. There is some evidence to show that women had been more fairly treated before the regulations of the Gortyn Code came into force. Although we cannot be certain, it may be, not only that women shared in the inheritance before the time of the Code, but that they had previously been entitled to a greater share, perhaps an equal share, with the brothers. In that case, the regulations of the Code in this connexion mark a further stage in the development of men's property rights over those of the women. By the fourth century B.C. it may also have been the case that daughters only received a dowry, fixed according to their sanctioned inheritance. According to Strabo, a girl's dowry was half of a brother's portion, if she had brothers.[11]

The Gortyn Code thus demonstrates the detailed legal attention now being paid, at the beginning of the fifth century B.C., to the safeguarding and transmission of the property rights which upheld the privileged position of the ruling citizen class. In addition to the citizens, there were three other main classes of the population; namely, the *apetairoi* (free persons excluded from political rights), the serfs and the slaves. The extent of the social privileges enjoyed by the ruling class of free citizens is exemplified by the following table showing the scale of fines for certain offences as detailed in the Gortyn Code.[12] The relative position of the various classes in the Cretan social hierarchy can be roughly assessed by a perusal of this tabulated evidence.

[11] *Ibid*. IV.23–V.9; Str. 10.482.  [12] *Leg.Gort*. II.2–16, 21–7.

A. *For rape:*

| | |
|---|---|
| 1. Against a free person | 1,200 obols |
| 2. Against an *apetairos* | 120 obols |
| 3. By a slave against a free person | 2,400 obols |
| 4. Against a serf by a free person | 30 obols |
| 5. Against a serf by a serf | 60 obols |
| 6. Against a household slave | 24, 1 or 2 obols depending on circumstances |

B. *For adultery:*

| | |
|---|---|
| 1. With a free woman | 600–1,200 obols |
| 2. With the wife of an *apetairos* | 120 obols |
| 3. A slave with a free woman | slave pays double (1,200–2,400 obols) |
| 4. Slave with slave | 60 obols |

It should be explained that rape, seduction and adultery were dealt with as offences of like category. That is to say, they were not looked upon as criminal, public wrong-doing but as matters to be settled by private monetary compensation. The scale of fines for adultery and rape were the same, with two exceptions. Adultery with a free woman led to the full fine of 1,200 obols only if the offence occurred in her father's, brother's or husband's house. The offence was considered less blameworthy if it occurred elsewhere and the fine was reduced by a half. Moreover, no mention is made of adultery between a free man and a serf's wife. We must assume that in such cases there was no legal redress.

By the time of the Code, adultery had become a civil wrong to be punished by fines and only concerned the individuals and their families. The offender was taken prisoner by the family affected by the wrong. His own family, if he was a free man, his master if he was not a free man, were told to ransom the prisoner within five days, failing which the captors would deal with him as they thought fit. However, if the person accused complained that he was the victim of a ruse, the matter was no longer dealt with by the family and the accuser had to swear to his testimony on oath. Later on, we know that the procedure thus outlined in the Gortyn Code had been changed. For the state took over, probably by the following century, the punishment of the offence of adultery. The accused was then made to appear before the magistrates. Upon conviction, he had to pay a fine to the state, lost his civil rights and was denied public employment.[13]

[13] *Ibid.* II.28–36; Ael. *VH* 12.12.

94

# VII

✦✦✦✦✦✦✦✦✦✦✦✦✦✦✦✦✦✦✦✦✦✦

## Serfs and Slaves

✦✦✦✦✦✦✦✦✦✦✦✦✦✦✦✦✦✦✦✦✦✦

T H E use of iron as a basic metal in the Greek city-states raised the general level of productivity and, as was mentioned earlier, commodity production was stimulated to such a degree that Greek society was the first to become based upon a monetary economy. In fact, the central feature of the whole process of development of the city-states is the growth of commodity production. As the basis of production changed, the social institutions changed accordingly, including the various types of servitude which had become essential to their maintenance. The slave systems of Greek antiquity developed over a long period of time and many problems associated with their genesis and growth still remain to be solved. Their later stages of development, especially in Athens, are better documented than their less mature phases. However, over the past few decades more attention has been directed by scholars to the early stages and their associated problems. As a result, it has at least become clear that the development of slavery was as uneven a process as the historical development of the city-states themselves. In this kind of investigation, the servile system of historical Crete is of major importance. For in Crete the aristocracy continued to maintain a dominant position because the early form of patriarchal slavery, which we can properly define as serfdom (with the peasants tied to the soil and paying tribute to overlords), persisted for centuries after commercial chattel slavery (with the slaves being bought and sold like other commodities), had become the dominating form of servitude in other city-states.

Crete was similar to Sparta in the sense that their systems of serfdom maintained the production of direct means of subsistence. Tribute in kind was exacted under the authority of the state. But Aristotle, as we saw, praised the more communal system of the Cretans, by which all citizens were supported from public resources, to which the regular tributes from the serfs were contributed. From what Dosiadas tells us of Lyttos, we can see that rent in kind could also be supplemented by money-rent, since the Lyttian serfs were compelled to contribute one stater per head. The Cretan aristocratic régimes, supported by this form of servitude, continued with relative stability until Hellenistic times; and when they did become unstable, they were transformed not by a process of radical change from within, but as a result of foreign conquest. However, with the introduction of a monetary system, the way was prepared for the gradual disintegration of the old collective system of land tenure and the emergence of the autonomous family based upon private property. Already in the Gortyn Code a premium was being set upon the division of property, even though there was no free testamentary disposition as yet and landed wealth was still supreme. But a monetary system eventually brought about the alienation of estates. On the testimony of Polybios this had become general by Hellenistic times. For there is no evidence to deny his statement that the laws of the Cretans allowed them to possess as much land as they could possibly acquire. When the landed estates did pass into private ownership, the peasant serfs also presumably became privately owned. However, we have no information as to how this change of ownership affected their social status and conditions. Even so, common ownership was not entirely superseded by private ownership. For there is a certain amount of evidence to show that individual cities continued to have public land at their disposal even in Roman times.[1]

Of course, the transition from collective tenure of the estates to individual ownership must have caused modifications in the serf system from time to time and probably from place to place.

[1] Rostovteff, SEHRE 274; Willetts, ASAC 44, 135, 253 n. 1.

No doubt too it was affected by the simultaneous development of chattel slavery. Hence the ancient evidence of terminology relating to the servile population is complex, varied and difficult to analyse. [2]

Thus, for example, the Gortyn Code has two servile terms (*woikeus* i.e. person attached to the household, the *oikos*) and *dolos* (i.e. slave) which we can properly render as 'serf' and 'slave'. But the two words are not strictly used to connote two different conditions of servility. Yet it is clear from various contexts in the Code that two different servile conditions obtained, and the word *dolos* sometimes has the same meaning as *woikeus*, though elsewhere it means a chattel slave. As we saw at the end of the last chapter, for instance, a penalty was laid down for rape against a domestic slave, so that one rule applied to a serf and another to a slave. The Code therefore, at this point, examined in order cases where the victim of rape was (a) a free citizen, (b) an *apetairos*, (c) a serf and (d) a slave, the fines applicable to the offences showing in the clearest terms the sharp differences which existed in social status.

The Gortyn Code also contains evidence to show that a free citizen could pledge his person as security for the payment of a debt. When he did so he was then called a *katakeimenos*, while a *nenikamenos* was a free man who had been condemned for debt and subsequently handed over in bondage to his creditor. Although such people were certainly no longer considered as free citizens, they were equally certainly not reduced to the lowest category of chattel slaves. The opening regulations of the Code are concerned with disputes over ownership of servile persons or those alleged to be servile. These regulations can be quoted here to illustrate the immediate context and also to exemplify the way in which the Code normally expresses its sanctions:

'Whosoever may be likely to contend about a free man or a slave is not to seize him before trial. But, if he make seizure, let the judge condemn him to a fine of ten staters for a free man, five for a slave of whomsoever he does seize and let him give judgement that he release him within three days. But if he do not release him, let the judge condemn him to a fine of a stater for a free man and a drachma for a slave, for each day until he do

[2] Cf. Lotze, MEKD; Finley, SSAG.

release him; and the judge is to decide on oath as to the time. But if he should deny the seizure, unless a witness should testify, the judge is to decide on oath. And if one party contend that he is a free man, the other party that he is a slave, whichever persons testify that he is a free man are to prevail. And if they contend about a slave, each declaring that he is his, the judge is to give judgement according to the witness if a witness testify, but he is to decide on oath if they testify either for both or for neither. After the one in possession has been defeated, he is to release the free man within five days and give back the slave in hand. But if he should not release or give back, let the judge give judgement that the successful party be entitled, in the case of the free man to fifty staters and a stater for each day until he releases him, in the case of the slave ten staters and a drachma for each day until he gives him back in hand. But at a year's end after the judge has pronounced judgement, the three-fold fines are to be exacted, or less, but not more. As to the time, the judge shall decide under oath. But if the slave on whose account a man has been defeated take sanctuary in a temple, the defeated party, summoning the successful party in the presence of two free adult witnesses, shall point him out at the temple where he takes refuge, either himself or another for him; and if he do not summon or point out, let him pay what is written. But if he should not give him back at all within the yearly period, he shall in addition pay the single penalties. If the defeated party die while the suit is being tried, he shall pay the single penalty. And if one who is *kosmos* make a seizure or another seize the slave of one who is *kosmos*, they are to contend after he resigns, and, if defeated, he shall pay what is written from the day he made the seizure. But one who seizes a man condemned for debt or who has mortgaged his person (i.e. a *nenikamenos* or a *katakeimenos*) shall be immune from punishment.'[3]

When a case was pending then, the person in dispute could not be seized before the trial. But the *katakeimenos* and the *nenikamenos* could be seized. This meant that the creditor was allowed to take the initiative in securing the services of the bonded person; and a clear distinction in status was thus implied.

Other information from inscriptional evidence at Gortyn helps to clarify this status further. The man who did mortgage

---

[3] *Leg.Gort.* I.1–II.2.

his person could not be penalized if he did something wrong which resulted in a loss to the creditor to whom he was in bondage, if it could be proved that the creditor was the instigator. Again, if he committed some trespass against a third person, he had to pay the penalty and not his temporary master; and if he was not able to pay, the third party and his master made some kind of arrangement. Hence a man who had thus mortgaged his person could defend himself at law, though he could not take independent action on his own account. If he did want to seek redress for some wrong committed against him, his master could press an action on his behalf. Any fine awarded in consequence of such a legal proceeding had to be the same as that awarded to a free man, but the master took half of it. If his master took no action on his behalf, he was allowed to initiate legal proceedings himself once his period of bondage was terminated.[4]

It seems also that the term *katakeimenos* could signify not only a man who mortgaged his person but also a slave given in pledge. Both the former and the temporary owner were responsible for the actions of such a person, since he was not recognized by the law as a responsible person in his own right. This contrast in the attitude of the law is revealing. For it means that the man who mortgaged his person and the man condemned for debt were recognized as having a higher status than the chattel slave. Their status in fact can be compared with that of the serf (*woikeus*) of the Gortyn Code, who had the right of access to the law-courts, even though the likelihood is that he was represented in legal proceedings by his master. It seems reasonable to suppose that his rights at law were less than the rights of a free man, because the initiative in any legal proceedings had to be taken by the master.[5]

The serfs possessed other social rights which further distinguished their status from that of chattel slaves. For they had the right of tenure of the houses, and also the contents of those houses, in which they lived. Such houses were looked upon, just like the serfs themselves, as part of the ancestral estates. Serfs too were able to possess cattle in their own right. Also they must surely have possessed money to be able to pay the fines assessed for offences enumerated in the Gortyn Code. For

[4] *Inscr. Cret.* 4.41. V–VI.    [5] Willetts, ASAC 55–6.

example, the divorced wife who exposed her child before pre-
senting it as the law prescribed had to pay a fine of fifty staters
if the child was free; and half that amount if the child was servile.
The mother here must have been a serf and not a slave. Again,
when the slave is taken in adultery with the wife of a slave, the
word for slave here (*dolos*) must mean 'serf', because legal
marriage was presumably not allowed between chattel slaves.
All this evidence apart, there is the evidence of Dosiadas to the
effect that the serfs of Lyttos contributed a stater per head by
way of tribute.

The serf family held a recognized social and legal status, the
serf being allowed both to marry and divorce. The serf's wife,
moreover, was entitled to possession of her own property, that
is to say, of movables, including livestock, which reverted to
her charge in case of divorce. When the serf woman married,
she changed masters. If she was divorced, she either returned
to her former master or to his relatives. It was assumed that the
master had a right to a child when both its parents were his
serfs. When a female serf had a child after being divorced, she
was obliged to take it to the master of her former husband. If
he did not want to have the child, it then became the concern of
her own master. The master of the husband was guaranteed
the right to the serf child if the divorced couple decided to re-
marry within a year. As we have seen, regular marriages were
allowed between free women and male serfs, though not apparently between free men and serf women.

If a serf became a runaway from the estate to which he was
bound, it seems likely that he sacrificed his social and legal rights
and could then be sold as a slave by his master, subject to certain
delays which were enforced by the law.

In different circumstances, however, the serf's status could be
more favourably affected by the law. As we saw, according to the
Gortyn Code, when a man or woman died and left no children,
the right of inheritance passed first of all to nearer relatives and,
failing that, to the clansmen. But if there were none of these,
the right of inheritance then passed to what the Code defines as
'those of the household composing the *klaros* (estate)', which
means the serfs who were bound to the ancestral estate of the
deceased. Parallels to this remarkable ultimate right of tenure
can be cited from other parts of Greece in antiquity and they

help to suggest, although we cannot precisely specify the status of such masterless servile inheritors, that one possible consequence was that they were freed from the direct obligation of tribute in kind. Hasluck reported an analogous situation from more recent times, describing how the Greek villagers of Kouvouklia were said to be the descendants of Peloponnesian immigrants who were settled in the time of Sultan Suleiman the Magnificent (1520–66) as serfs on the lands of the local derebey, Karadja Oghlu. These serfs gradually acquired land, and at the death of the last derebey, about the middle of last century, when there was no direct heir, they were left in possession after a long lawsuit.

This clearly recognized status of the Cretan serfs must have derived from the authority of age-old custom, which may well have gone back to Minoan times. This is what can be inferred from the remark of Aristotle that the laws of Minos were still in force among the subject population of Crete.[6]

When we compare the evidence of the Gortyn Code with what Polybios tells us about land tenure, we can measure the extent of the development of private property after coined money had been introduced in the early fifth century B.C. One possible consequence of this development has been mentioned, namely that, in some parts of Crete at some time, at least, the serfs on what became privately owned, as opposed to collectively owned, estates, became subjected to a form of private servitude. It is impossible, however, to say how their former status was changed when they did thus become privately owned and the extent to which it approximated to the status of the chattel slave.

Until such a change did occur anywhere in Crete, the condition of the peasants remained as it had been for centuries past. The cultivators lived on the ancestral estates of Dorian rulers, which had been allotted, in consequence of tribal custom, among the households. Bound to these estates, the serfs were compelled to pay tribute. Their status was comparable with that of the Spartan helots and other peasant classes elsewhere in the Greek world. This status was set somewhere between that of the full citizen on the one hand and that of the chattel slave on the other. The serf's bondage was characteristic of landed wealth, the

6 *Leg.Gort.* III–V, VII; *Inscr. Cret.* 4.41.IV; Hasluck, 149; Arist. *Pol.* 1271 b 30.

chattel's inferior status characteristic of an urban, money economy.

This distinction is pointed in a fragmentary reference to Crete by Kallistratos[7] who tells us that the Cretans called their urban slaves *chrysonetoi*, that is, 'persons bought for gold', a term which is coloured by the relative novelty of buying and selling for ready money, which has become a commonplace for us, though it was not so in the Classical age of Greece. This Cretan term for a chattel carried with it the implication that something which should not be bought and sold had been shamefully acquired for money.

Chattel slaves then, as distinct from the serfs, formed the lowest section of the community. Serfs, like the land they lived upon and worked, were inalienable until the old system was disrupted by a money economy. Slaves, like other movables, were commodities to be bought and sold, their value assessed according to the fluctuations of the open market. When the Gortyn Code prescribed that, when the master died and the heirs could not agree about their shares, the property should be sold and the proceeds divided, the property to be sold would include any slaves. In the same way, when the heiress was allowed to possess the town-house and everything in the house, the slaves would be included, like the furniture. Both serf and slave had a master. But their different economic status gave them different places in the social hierarchy.

[7] *Ap*. Ath. 6.263 e–f.

# VIII

❖❖❖❖❖❖❖❖❖❖❖❖❖❖❖❖❖❖❖❖❖❖❖❖❖❖❖❖❖❖❖❖❖❖❖❖❖

## Other Social Classes

❖❖❖❖❖❖❖❖❖❖❖❖❖❖❖❖❖❖❖❖❖❖❖❖❖❖❖❖❖❖❖❖❖❖❖❖❖

Between the small class of privileged free citizens on the one hand and the servile classes on the other, there existed a number of other social groups whose exact status is very difficult to define because of the fragmentary nature of the available evidence.

We saw[1] that the *apetairoi* constituted such a group, being free persons in the sense that they were neither bonded nor enslaved. In fact, the name given to them signifies that they were excluded from the *hetaireiai*, the closed corporations of male citizens, and therefore from the privileges bestowed by membership of these bodies, in particular, of course, the political rights of citizenship. It is therefore possible that they included the members of various communities which were subject to one or another of the city-states but possessed some kind of autonomy. For example, in an early fifth-century B.C. inscription from Gortyn, a man named Dionysios was granted certain privileges which included exemption from taxation, the right to sue in the same courts as citizens, and a house and land in Aulon. It has been suggested that Aulon was a community subject to Gortyn, with its own local government and taxes.

Another document suggests that the Gortynians had subjected the neighbouring city of Rhittenia, on the northern route

[1] P. 93.

to the sea. The document is a decree which begins by obliging
the people of Rhittenia to send to Mount Ida, on the occasion of
the triennial festival at the cave of Zeus, for which the Gortynians seem to have been responsible, three hundred and fifty
staters' worth of victims, or victims and money. Despite their
subjection, the Rhittenians were allowed their own laws and
courts, as the decree makes clear. The Gortynians were forbidden to take securities in the territory of Rhittenia. If anyone
contravened this sanction, he had to pay twice the value of the
security. The fine was to be imposed by the *kosmoi* of Rhittenia.
If the *kosmoi* failed to take action, the elders could exact from the
*kosmoi*. Gortynians could apparently buy and sell houses and
trees in Rhittenia, and Rhittenians at Gortyn. However, it is
made clear that a Rhittenian had the status of a foreigner at
Gortyn.

There is some evidence to suggest that the city of Eleutherna
exercised authority over some people called the Artemitai, in
the third century B.C. These Artemitai, who may have been
somehow connected with the cult of Artemis at Eleutherna,
were, so it seems, a subjected civic community, a village perhaps
or even a group of villages near to Eleutherna.

Evidence from the Hellenistic period shows that Gortyn
maintained relations with various cities in the south-west. In
particular there were relations of a special kind between Gortyn
and an island off the south-west coast, called Kaudos. It is
likely that these relations were established before the second
century B.C., but an important decree of the Gortynians concerning Kaudos survives from the beginning of that century and
indicates that Kaudos was subject to Gortyn, yet had some kind
of local self-government. In the decree the Kaudians were to pay
a tithe on all their products by land and sea, with the exception
of flocks, vegetables and harbour-dues. In addition to this tribute, the people of Kaudos were to send quantities of salt and
juniper berries to Gortyn.

The glimpses we get from scattered evidence of this kind into
the conditions of subject communities enables us to arrive at
some rough notion of what was entailed in the status of being
less than a citizen and more than a serf.

We can speculate further by supposing that other groups who
were denied the privilege of membership of the *hetaireiai* were

looked upon as belonging to the category of *apetairoi*. For example, the serfs who assumed tenure of estates in the absence of other heirs could have assumed the status of *apetairoi*. Members of the citizen class who for one reason or another had been deprived of their civic rights might also have become *apetairoi*. So might the sons of a male citizen and a female slave or even the children of a free mother by a serf.

Freedmen and resident aliens (metics) were also, of course, excluded from membership of the *hetaireiai* of the citizens. But they were not *apetairoi*. For the resident aliens were under the jurisdiction of special courts for foreigners and also of the special magistrate appointed to deal with aliens (the *ksenios kosmos*). Freedmen too were officially regarded as being in the same sort of position as resident aliens, perhaps because they were all alike artisans.

Documentary evidence from Gortyn at the beginning of the fifth century B.C. appears to indicate that resident aliens and freedmen lived in a special area of the city called Latosion, the inhabitants being known as Latosioi. It may be that there was, in this old quarter of the city, a sanctuary of the goddess Lato and that special rights of responsibility for it were exercised by the state. In one document freedmen were given the same rights as the resident aliens of Latosion. Their legal status as relatively privileged members of the community was recognized, including immunity from arbitrary seizure. Nevertheless, their confinement to a special quarter deprived them of unrestricted movement and also, probably, of freedom of economic activity.[2]

Plato and Aristotle made remarks concerning resident aliens and freedmen which throw light upon their social status in general. Plato in the *Laws* writes: 'Whoever wishes may take up residence as an alien on fixed conditions, since residence is allowed to a foreigner who is both willing and able to reside as an alien, provided that he is skilled in some craft and remains in the state for not more than twenty years from the date of his registration, without even the payment of any small alien's tax —except for virtuous behaviour—or any tax for buying and selling. When his time expires, he is to go away and take his property with him. But if within the period of twenty years it transpires that he proves of special merit by doing some

[2] *Inscr. Cret.* 4.58, 64, 80, 184; *ibid.* 2.XII 22 B.

outstanding service to the state and he believes that he can persuade the Council and Assembly to grant his request for postponement of his departure or even an extension of his residence for life, whatever request he succeeds in persuading the state to grant to him shall be carried out to the limit. For the children of resident aliens, who are craftsmen and over fifteen years of age, the period of alien residence shall begin from the fifteenth year and such a person, after remaining for twenty years, shall go where he pleases or, should he wish to remain, he shall seek permission in the same way. Anyone who goes must first cancel the entries previously made by him in the register kept by the magistrates.'[3]

Aristotle stated that craftsmen, i.e. free artisans, were in a condition of limited slavery. Elsewhere he elaborates this view in a passage that has a special relevance for Crete: 'Just as there are several kinds of constitution, there must likewise be several kinds of citizen, and especially of the citizen in a subject position. Therefore in one constitution the craftsman and the hired labourer will be citizens, in other constitutions this will be impossible, for example in any kind of aristocratic constitution in which honours are bestowed according to virtue and worth. For a person who lives a craftsman's life or the life of a hired labourer cannot practise the pursuits which have to do with virtue.'[4]

Some regulations envisaged by Plato in a passage of the *Laws* illustrate the limited degrees of freedom allowed to manumitted slaves in the Greek cities: 'A man may arrest a freedman too (i.e. as well as a slave), should the freedman not attend upon or inadequately attend upon, those who have emancipated him. This attendance shall consist in the coming of the emancipated person three times a month to the home of the man who emancipated him, undertaking to perform those duties which are both just and practicable, and to behave in the matter of his marriage too as may seem proper to his former master. The freedman is not to be allowed to be more wealthy than the man who emancipated him. Any excess is to be handed over to his former master. Such a freedman is not to remain in the state for more than twenty years, but is to go away like all other foreigners, taking with him all of his property—unless he can prevail upon the magistrates and the man who emancipated him.'[5]

---

[3] *Lg.* 850 a–c.    [4] *Pol.* 1260 b I; *ibid.* 1278 a 15–22.    [5] *Lg.* 915 a–b.

Such obligations upon a freedman to continue in service, representing a kind of deferred manumission, were often written into the many manumission agreements which have survived from Delphi. The manumitted slave agreed to continue to perform certain services for his former master, these services most frequently being obligatory during the lifetime of the owner who had sold his slave in trust to the god. These obligations were, in fact, usually reduced to periods of from two to ten years. In temple manumissions of this kind the obligatory services were part of the payment made by the emancipated person for his liberty. By such agreements the freedman had to go on living in the city of the ex-master so as to carry out his obligations.

With this general background in mind we can better understand a number of documents from Cretan cities concerning resident aliens and freedmen, including the Latosioi of Gortyn mentioned above. Two other documents from Gortyn of the fifth century B.C. are also relevant in this connexion. The earlier of the two is the end of some kind of decree which defined relations between the state and some craftsmen, or hired workmen, either resident aliens or freedmen. Rations of barley, figs, wine and other things were mentioned, which perhaps formed the annual rations of each man. The same pay was fixed for freedmen (or freemen—the inscription is mutilated at this point and we cannot be certain) and for slaves working in the city. Refusal to work incurred a fine of ten staters payable to the state and exacted by the *ksenios kosmos*. Double the amount was exacted if the simple fine was not paid. The later inscription is similar in purport. Provisions were allotted by annual amounts, payment was arranged on the same basis and the same penalty was laid down for any infringement.

An inscription from the city of Axos (sixth–fifth centuries B.C.) makes it reasonably certain that conditions were therein laid down between the state and some workers who may have come in or been brought in from outside. It appears that these workers were to be fed at public expense and were to be granted exemption from certain tributes. Another inscription from the city of Eleutherna (sixth?–fifth centuries B.C.) mentions a special category of workmen, presumably makers of goat's hair cloaks, and may have contained regulations for their pay.

It is possible that the free artisans mentioned in these documents were freedmen, at least in the case of Gortyn, if not of Axos and Eleutherna. In the case of the Gortynian evidence, the juxtaposition of freedmen (or freemen) and slaves in the terms of payment as well as the formulation of the clause defining the penalty for not doing the work lead us to suspect that the work was being done as some kind of forced labour. Men who were not slaves but were at the same time subject to compulsory obligations of this kind were presumably freedmen, perhaps inhabitants of Latosion. Because their rations were assessed on an annual basis, these workers might have been freedmen who were bound to service over a long period, the service being part of the terms of their manumission.

These terms of manumission, entailing a continued bondage service, could well have been arranged by the civil authorities, as opposed to trust purchases through a god, unless we are to suppose that some special significance attached to the fact that freedmen lived in Latosion, a place called after a goddess. For the documents define relations between freedmen and the state. We cannot, however, thereby suppose that the freedmen were originally owned by the state. As we saw, Plato envisaged the freedman as subject to state regulations and at the same time liable to render services to his former master.

The residential quarter for freedmen of Gortyn, known as Latosion, can be regarded as an early manifestation of the tendency, which was fully developed under the Roman Empire, for the state to bind craftsmen groups, as well as peasants, to fixed localities. We are also reminded that the 'guild' had origins reaching back into the Bronze Age. It is also interesting to see that freedmen were classed with resident aliens as inferiors of artisan status and that the growth of chattel slavery was beginning to affect adversely the status of the artisan, since he could be obliged to work at servile rates of pay.[6]

Several Gortynian decrees of manumission have survived from the Hellenistic period. They are all civil acts of manumission and several of them concern public slaves who were freed by the state. There are two others which deal with the manumission of the slaves of private individuals. Some of them make mention of the payment of a tax of manumission to the state within a

[6] Westermann, BSF 217; *Inscr. Cret.* 2.V.1, *ibid.* XII.9; *ib.* 4. 79, 144.

period of twelve days. All of the decrees were found at the site of the modern village of Mitropolis. Hence the suggestion that this village was also the site of ancient Latosion.[7]

All this evidence goes to show that freedmen were a distinct class of people at the same level of importance to the community as resident aliens.

[7] *Inscr. Cret.* 4.231–6.

# IX

## Education

THE ancient Greek city-states developed a variety of educational systems, more or less advanced according to the complexity of their social and political organization. But they have certain common features which show that they rested upon a primitive tribal basis. The Athenian system was the most highly developed and the one which has most influenced later educational theory. In Athens there continued to be two main branches of education, music and gymnastic. The term 'music' meant any art presided over by the Muses, particularly lyric poetry as well as music proper. Physical education took place in a gymnasium or a more modest building called a *palaistra* ('training-school'). The gymnasia were large and costly public buildings, of which even Athens possessed only three in the fourth century B.C. They were frequented by citizens of all ages, taking exercises themselves or watching others, and were centres of social and intellectual life. The gymnasium, in fact, typified a continued relationship between intellectual and physical education.

Eventually there were three stages of formal education in Athens. The primary stage lasted from the age of six to fourteen, the secondary stage from fourteen to eighteen, and the third from eighteen to twenty. This third stage was made compulsory by the state and here we find the closest parallels with the more rudimentary systems of the Dorian communities of Sparta and Crete and the closest formal links with primitive institutions. The young men of Athens, between the ages of eighteen and twenty, were a separate division of the community and they were called by the special term *epheboi* ('youths'). In the Classical period the ephebic system was an organized form of military training controlled by the state authorities. As soon as they were eighteen the young men entered upon their initiation into the duties and responsibilities of citizenship. If there was no doubt about his age and his parentage a young man's name was entered upon the register of his district. He was then legally an *ephebos* and took an oath of allegiance, probably after being instructed in the laws of the city. The various tribes of Athens each chose three men above the age of forty. One of these was eventually selected by the assembled people to supervise the *epheboi* of each tribe. They were responsible for morality and discipline, while military training was the responsibility of military officers. After this, the *epheboi* toured the temples, were put into garrisons and started their training. The *epheboi* of each tribe took their meals together. At the end of the first year, they received a spear and shield from the state and these were regarded as sacred. They spent the second year patrolling the frontier and manning forts. So long as they were *epheboi* the young men wore a special cloak, as did their Spartan and Cretan counterparts. There is reason to believe that the wearing of this cloak was connected with the age-old belief in the death of the child at initiation.

It is the purpose of tribal initiation to admit the child to the status of an adult. Just as a newly born child is looked upon as a re-born ancestor, so a child at puberty is considered to die as a child and to be born again as an adult. In the same way adults become transformed into elders and elders die to enter the highest of all grades, that of the totemic ancestors, who eventually are themselves re-born to begin the whole cyclic process anew.

This cyclic process, with its totemic background, accounts for the system of age-grades which we find in Sparta and in a less elaborate form in Crete, as well as the apparently extraordinary custom of naming certain social institutions as if they were intended for cattle rather than men.

Spartan education was essentially physical education and after his sixth year a Spartan boy started his progress through the different age-grades. For when he was seven he left home to live communally with other boys. It seems that boys of different ages were supervised by a young man called an *eiren*. They took their meals and slept together as members of what was called an *agela* ('herd'). These groupings crossed the groupings into age-classes. Each age-class was divided into *bouai* ('herds of oxen'), with *bouagoi* ('herd-leaders') of the same age. During the six-year period which lasted until he had completed his twelfth year, the boy went through the initial stages of the strict Spartan training, though not participating in competitive exercises in music, dancing or athletics until he was ten years old.

The next six-year period, the period of adolescence, lasted from 13 to 18. When this began, the boys shaved their heads and wore only one cloak, in summer and in winter. When they were eighteen, the boys became *melleirenes* and were candidates for the rank of *eiren*, attained in their nineteenth year. The *melleirenes* had to undergo an ordeal, a common feature of initiation rites into manhood. This took the form of a public scourging at the altar of the goddess Artemis Orthia and we know that the ceremony was continued until the fourth century A.D. At the end of his twenty-fourth year the Spartan became a first line-soldier, a full citizen and therefore a member of the Assembly when he was thirty; and it was not until he was thirty that he could live with his wife and family. Between the ages of about eighteen and twenty, the Spartan youths were organized into what was called the *krypteia*, sometimes translated as 'secret police' or 'secret service'. This service is likely to have involved a period of withdrawal from ordinary social life to the seclusion of the country districts. Such a period of withdrawal is also a common feature of the stages of initiation from boyhood to manhood in tribal communities and it is this notion of withdrawal which may account for the clandestine associations of the word *krypteia*. The girls of Sparta were also organized in 'herds' like the boys.

With these parallels in mind we can better assess the evidence that has survived concerning the education system of Crete. In the sphere of education, as in other spheres of social life, it is fair to say that the customs of Doric tribalism had become more modified through the centralized state apparatus in Crete than in Sparta. Though these tribal customs had become more attenuated, there is no evidence that the education system controlled by the state authorities had been influenced by the enlightenment of the democratic cities.

Fewer age-grade terms have survived from Crete as compared with Sparta, except those relating to puberty and the crucial initiatory transition period from youth to manhood. The Gortyn Code contains a number of age-grades applied to the free citizens, including *anoros* or *anebos* to mean those below the age of puberty, and *ebion*, *ebionsa* and *orima* those after the age of puberty. Two other names illustrate the part played by foot-racing in the traditions of the social community. The term *dromeus* ('runner') was given to an adult citizen after the age probably of about twenty and implied that the citizen had the right of access to the public gymnasium—a right which, as we saw, was denied to the serf class. Conversely, the term *apodromos* was used of a minor, implying that he did not yet possess the right to participate in public athletic exercises.[1]

The young men of the Cretan cities, like the Spartans, were organized in 'herds'. We know from Strabo[2] that those who graduated from the 'herds' were obliged to marry at the same time. Thus Cretan marriage was a public, state-controlled ceremony, involving those who belonged to the same age-grade and who, as we have seen, also belonged to groups which had compacts of intermarriage with other groups. This ancient tribal custom persisted for long despite the disruptive tendencies based on more recent developments associated with private property and the autonomous family. These tendencies had begun to operate by the time of the Gortyn Code in which an exception was made to the general rule of collective marriage in the case of the minor who was allowed to marry the heiress to safeguard the interests of the household despite the prevalence of ancient custom. For the need to ensure succession in the male line explains the fact that the Gortynian heiress could be married at the early age of twelve, and also the right of a minor to marry an heiress as an exception to the old rule.

The special term *apageloi* was probably restricted to adolescents in the period immediately prior to their entry into the

---

[1] *Leg.Gort. passim.*, Willetts, ASAC 7–17.      [2] 10.482.

'herd'. Though the Cretan 'herds' were similar to the bands of
citizen novices in other states, the youths did not form their own
'herds' until the end of their seventeenth year. Therefore an
*apagelos* was a boy not yet belonging to an *agela* ('herd'). But
we also know that *apageloi* could be described as *skotioi* ('secret
ones'). The most likely interpretation of this term is that it was
apt for those who were about to be involved in the various
initiatory rites and customs associated with the transition from
youth to manhood, including a period of seclusion from the city
lasting for two months. Therefore the Cretan boys at this age
can be compared with the Spartans when they became old enough
for service with the *krypteia*. These facts enable us to explain
too why the goddess Aphrodite, patron goddess of youths who
were about to undertake initiation into citizenship and marriage,
was called, in the city of Phaistos, Aphrodite Skotia.[3]

Dosiadas tells us: 'Everywhere throughout Crete there are
two houses for the communal messes, one of them called
the *andreion* ("men's house"), the other the *koimeterion*
("sleeping-place"), in which they entertain strangers.' It may
be that the second of these was also used as a sleeping-place for
the young men. For when Ephoros explains that all the young
men were compelled to marry at the same time when they left
the 'herd', he adds that they did not immediately take their
wives to their own homes but only when they had learnt how
to manage household affairs. Since the young men belonged to
'herds', it is perhaps more likely that they slept in some such
place as the *koimeterion* rather than in their parents' homes.[4]

This inference is confirmed by what we know of the 'men's
house' from anthropological sources. This building is usually
the largest in a tribal community, belonging in common to the
people of a settlement, used as a council chamber, a guest-house
for strangers, a sleeping-quarter for the men, and a sort of club-
house for bachelors. Moreover, as Hutton Webster pointed out,[5]
the presence in a primitive community of the 'men's house' in
any one of its numerous forms, points strongly to the existence,
now or in the past, of secret initiation ceremonies.

The literary sources make it clear that the term *andreion* was
also applied to the *hetaireia* which foregathered there and also

[3] Hsch. *s.v.* ἀπάγελος; sch. E.*Alc.* 989; Willetts, CCF 175–9, 285–6.
[4] Dosiad. *ap.* Ath. 143; Ephor. *ap.* Str. 10.482.          [5] PSS 1f.

to the communal meals which the members of the *hetaireia* shared. When the youths passed out of the 'herds' they would normally become full members of these adult associations.[6]

Our chief literary source of information about Cretan educational training is from Ephoros as reported by Strabo. The boys, he writes, had to learn their letters and also lays from the laws and certain forms of music. Those still younger were taken to the communal meals, or 'clubs'. They sat together on the ground to eat their food, wearing shabby clothes, the same in summer as in winter, and waiting on the men as well as on themselves. Grouped according to 'clubs', with each group under the control of an instructor, they held contests with one another and with other 'clubs'. Older boys were taken into the 'herds'. These were organized by the most outstanding and influential of the young men, each of whom gathered together as many others as he could. The leader of each of the 'herds' was usually the father of the organizer, who had the authority to lead them out to hunt and to run races, and also to punish any of them who were disobedient. They were fed at the public expense. The 'herds' contended with one another in warlike exercises, which were accompanied, as in actual warfare, by the music of flutes and lyres.[7]

Thus education during childhood chiefly consisted of attendance at the communal meals of the men, there being no independent youth organizations until the end of the seventeenth year. There was certainly an early introduction to collective organization before then, and the essential features of their training generally seem to have been of a traditional kind, with restricted formal instruction, military education through physical exercises, music, warrior's songs, hunting and mock warfare, all under the general supervision of the adult males, and culminating in compulsory marriage with the ritual of initiation into citizenship and marriage. Thus, by the fourth century B.C., the old tribal customs had been relaxed considerably in certain respects as compared with the situation in Sparta, with individualism playing a distinctive part in the sense that the 'herds' had become, to a certain extent, private forms of organization, dependent upon the patronage of influential people. On the other hand the common obligation to marry was certainly an archaic custom hardly impaired by the changes apparent elsewhere.

[6] Jeanmaire, CC 423f.; Willetts, ASAC 18ff.      [7] 10.482–4.

The love affairs of the Cretan youths, as they are described by Ephoros, were also imbued with characteristically archaic features. They centred upon a kind of mock 'marriage' by abduction—but of a younger by an older boy. The boy's friends were told several days beforehand that the abduction was going to be carried out. It was considered disgraceful for these friends to conceal the boy or not to let him go out on to the appointed road, since this would have been a kind of admission that the boy was unworthy of the attachment. At the appointed time, if the abductor was the boy's equal or superior, either socially or in other respects, the friends of the boy pursued and laid hold of him, though only in a gentle sort of way, so as to satisfy tradition. Afterwards they cheerfully turned him over to the abductor to lead away. But if the abductor was an unworthy person, the boy's friends took him away.

The pursuit terminated when the boy was taken to the 'men's house' of the abductor. After he had given presents to the boy, the abductor took him away into the country. Those who were present at the abduction followed after them and joined them in feasting and hunting for two months. This was the prescribed period which could not be exceeded and afterwards they returned to the city. The boy was then released after he had received a number of presents according to custom. These traditional gifts, apart from other things so numerous and costly that all the friends helped to defray the expenses, consisted of a military dress, an ox and a drinking-cup. The ox was then sacrificed to Zeus by the young initiate, who gave a feast to those who had been his companions.

Such abducted boys were known as *parastathentes* ('those set beside') and they received special favours. They held the positions of highest honour in dances and races and were allowed to dress in better clothes than the others, the clothes presented to them by their abductors. When they were grown-up men even they wore a distinctive dress, signifying that they were distinguished persons.

These customs remind us of the common folklore story of the youth who is carried off from his parents by jealous divinities when he is to be initiated. Perhaps, too, the Cretan aristocrats of the historical period were imitating rites which were practised in some form by the élite band of youths who, Evans thought, existed at the court of Minos at Knossos in Bronze Age times—young initiates chosen for special office. Certainly the sacrifice of the ox may well derive from Minoan ritual.[8]

Some significance too attaches to the present of a warrior's dress. For the inscriptional evidence from various cities indicates that when the youths took part in the annual ceremony of graduation from the 'herds', that is to say, when they reached the culminating stage of their initiation into manhood, they cast aside their boys' clothes and took the warriors' garb which they received after their period of seclusion. The boy died and was re-born as a man, the change being marked by the casting-away of boys' clothes and the wearing of a mature citizen warrior's dress. For these annual festivals combined archaic elements of fertility-rites, initiation and marriage. Moreover, the aspect of regeneration was extended to the oaths taken at these annual ceremonies, whether oaths of personal loyalty or those appended to state treaties. Not only were the youths re-born as citizens; in a sense the life of the city was also renewed.[9]

We can estimate the importance which was attached to this training system, if we bear in mind what was happening elsewhere. In the third century B.C. the numbers of *epheboi* at Athens became quite small. Nor was the age qualification strictly observed. By the next century, foreigners were being incorporated and eventually native Athenians were in the minority. In the course of time, too, military training gave way to athletics and courses in literature, rhetoric and philosophy were instituted. Wealthy young men came to study in Athens, the leading university of the Roman Empire. The Athenian system of ephebic training thus became a university system of formal higher education.

The archaic system of grouping by age-classes continued in Hellenistic times and most Greek cities still had systems of ephebic training. But generally speaking, where the cities lost their independence to pass under the rule of monarchs who were served by standing armies, military training was no longer nearly so important in the educational system.

Crete, however, formed an exception to this general tendency, though the island certainly lost the isolation of former

[8] Evans, PM 4.397–9; Willetts, CCF 116–17.
[9] Willetts, CCF 306–7 *et passim*.

days, and was increasingly subjected to influences from without. But no federal organization came about and their cities held to their separatism until the Roman conquest. In these circumstances the 'herd' training of the youth was maintained as a prerequisite for admission into the citizen body. In fact, the aristocratic rulers not merely maintained, but extended their control over the training of the youth. There was continued marked emphasis on military training, which is not surprising since warfare was endemic between the cities. The traditional cults of the novices were also deliberately fostered as a means of supporting conservative institutions and preventing innovation in the political and social life of the city-states. The annual oath of the new citizens shows how they were put under binding obligations through the close relationship between the state and the official state religion.

Thus, in the Drerian oath of the late third or early second century B.C. (which has been noticed earlier[10]), the new citizens of Dreros swear loyalty to their own city and its ally, Knossos, and enmity to Lyttos. At this ceremonial oath-taking, the young men laid aside their boyhood clothes in the usual way and assumed their citizen warriors' garb. The document concludes with an archaic and obscure section, the purport of which appears to be that the youths were involved in an ordeal of initiation, which perhaps took the form of a race, from which one of them emerged as a victor, the winner and his competitors being placed under an obligation to cultivate an olive tree.

[10] P. 71.

# X

Religion

DESPITE the social changes which brought about modifications in the organization of the Cretan system of training their youth, that system preserved, with remarkable tenacity, particularly in its final stages, certain archaic features, including, as we saw, collective marriage. The Drerian oath shows that, even in the Hellenistic period, the training of the youth was still deeply imbued with ritualistic ideas based on initiation ceremonies and fertility cults. These survivals illustrate the most significant feature of Cretan religion throughout antiquity. The conventional Olympian pantheon of gods and goddesses was introduced into the official religion of the Cretan cities in the course of the first millennium B.C., as elsewhere throughout Greece, but not far below the surface, and indeed sometimes openly at the surface, survived myths, cults, beliefs and practices inherited from Minoan and even pre-Minoan times. /

The cult of Zeus Kretagenes—'Cretan-born' Zeus—is one such cult of great antiquity which also continued to flourish in Hellenistic times. In fact, this god's name of Zeus was presumably borrowed from the Greeks. What it was in Minoan times we do not know, but Guthrie has suggested that it was an Oriental name which travelled to Crete by way of Phoenicia, perhaps the name later Hellenized as Zagreus.[1]

[1] Guthrie, OGR 112–13; Cook, Z.1.651.

119

The myth of the birth of Cretan Zeus is told by the poet Hesiod in his *Theogony*. Before the age of the Olympians, the Titans, children of Heaven and Earth, were supreme. Kronos, the youngest of the Titans, married Rhea. Hestia, Demeter, Hera, Hades and Poseidon, their first children, were swallowed by Kronos, who feared that one or another of them might usurp his kingship. Consequently, before she gave birth to Zeus, she went to Lyttos in Crete to conceal the birth, on the advice of her parents. Rhea's mother took the baby Zeus to rear him in a deep cave on the wooded 'Goat-Mountain' (Aigaion). The baby was replaced by a stone wrapped in swaddling-clothes which Kronos swallowed, subsequently vomiting it up together with the children he had swallowed before.[2]

This stone which was substituted for Zeus is the thunder-stone, a further indication of the origin of the myth in the pre-historic stratum of Cretan religion. The 'Goat-Mountain' is related to the legend that the baby Zeus drank the milk of the goat Amaltheia. In general too, the myth is similar to many folk-tales centred upon the child abandoned by its mother and reared by others. In this respect the myth has the same background as the custom which required the Cretan initiates to hide themselves away in the country for some time before the initiation ceremony. The Kouretes of Crete, young men who, says Hesiod, were lovers of sport and dancing, danced, according to tradition, around the baby Zeus, beating drums and clashing spears on their shields to drown its cries from the ears of Kronos. The Kouretes were, as Jane Harrison explained, initiated young men personified. It was natural for them to be associated with the birth and nurture of the baby Zeus.[3]

The Cretan-born Zeus, Zeus Kretagenes, was also known as Diktaian Zeus in the eastern part of the island. This epithet derived from the Diktaian Cave on Mount Dikte where the god was supposed to have been born and nourished either by bees, or a goat, or a pig or doves and entrusted to the Kouretes or to the Korybantes, who were identified with them. One of the most important festivals in this part of Crete was known as the Thiodaisia. The evidence shows that it was customary at this festival to renew the oaths of alliance between cities; and also that the ritual graduation of the youths from the 'herds' was

[2] Hes. *Th.* 453ff.        [3] Harrison, T.19, *56*; Willetts, CCF 213 n. 93.

associated with it. Since the festival was an occasion of initiation and renewal of life, the city's birthday was celebrated, and its oaths of alliance were renewed as well as its own citizen body.

This festival was the equivalent of the Athenian Dionysia, for the Cretan Zeus was like Dionysos in all essentials. The festival at Athens lasted for nearly a week. The image of Dionysos was carried in procession from the city on the first day to a shrine on the road to the village of Eleutherai, its supposed original home, on the frontier between Attica and Boiotia. It was escorted by armed *epheboi*. The image was placed on a low altar, hymns were sung in praise of the god and animals were sacrificed, in particular a bull, which was chosen as being 'worthy of the god' and sacrificed on behalf of the state. The bull was then presumably roasted and the meat shared among the state officials. After the feast, the procession returned to the city by torchlight in the evening. The *epheboi* took the image of Dionysos to the theatre, where it rested on an altar in the middle of the orchestra for the duration of the festival.

These events of the first day of the festival followed a three-fold ritual sequence familiar in tribal initiations, where the initiate is taken away from his home, goes through an ordeal and comes back as a man. The abducted Cretan boys went away from the city with their fellow-initiates, stayed hunting and feasting for a time and then returned, for the abducted boy to receive his presents of a military dress, a drinking-cup and an ox. The Cretan initiates were the equivalent of the Athenian *epheboi* who also took part in a procession from the city and a triumphal return. The bull 'worthy of the god' was likely to have been regarded as the actual incarnation of the god. The sacrifice of the bull was then the ordeal, the ordeal of the god.

The Olympic festival had the same threefold pattern as its basis, but here the ordeal took the form of athletic contests. Of these the men's foot-race was originally a ritual ordeal of initiation to decide the champion youth of the year, who was invested with magical powers lasting from seed-time to harvest. These ideas of primitive magic explain the honours which were still bestowed on the Olympian victors in historical times. They were crowned with olive and feasted in the town-hall at Olympia. When they returned to their cities they were clad in purple and drawn by white horses in procession through a breach in the walls. Spartan victors marched beside their boys to ensure victory in battle. The Athenian victors ate at public cost for their lifetime and were worshipped as heroes after death. It is not surprising that there was a local tradition at Olympia that the Kouretes came there from Crete and ran a race.

The special deity honoured at the Cretan Thiodaisia, associated with initiation into citizenship and collective marriage of the new citizens, presumably originated from the Minoan bull-god who later became linked with Zeus—but a Cretan-born Zeus. Foot-races must have featured prominently in the 'ordeal' part of this festival and a bull-sacrifice probably played a part of equal importance. The archaic ending of the Drerian oath shows how magical tributes still attached to the victor of the ordeal. The competitors in this ordeal had to tend and cultivate olives. We are reminded that when the Kouretes came from Crete to run at Olympia, tradition said that the winner was crowned with wild olive. Likewise, olives stood at the end of the Athenian race-course.

This aspect of the ordeal, with all its magical and fertility associations, helps us to understand why a citizen was called a 'runner' (*dromeus*) and why, in one Hellenistic inscription from the city of Lato, the citizen novices are referred to as those who 'run out'.[4]

The attitude of such youthful novices to their patron deity is revealed in the famous Hymn of the Kouretes in honour of Diktaian Zeus, discovered at the site of his temple at Palaikastro in eastern Crete.[5] The inscription was probably made as late as the third century A.D., but the original was much older. For it was inscribed twice on the same stone, first badly and then more correctly. We assume therefore that it must have been copied either from some existing written record or from oral tradition.

The hymn takes the form of a series of stanzas and a recurrent refrain. The text of the refrain and the first stanza are complete and can be translated thus:

> O hail, thou Kronian,
> O welcome, greatest Kouros,
> Almighty of Brightness,

[4] *Inscr. Cret.* I.XVI.5.
[5] *Ibid.*, 3.II.2; bibliography and discussion in Willetts, CCF 211ff.

Here now present, leading thy spirits,
O come for the year to Dikte,
And rejoice in this ode,

Which we on the strings strike, as we
Blend it with the pipes' sounds, as we
Are chanting our song, standing round
This thy altar, walled so well.

The hymn may well have been sung by the novices from the
'herd' as part of a festival like the Thiodaisia to honour the
epiphany of Cretan-born Zeus. Since the Cretan *parastathentes*
sacrificed oxen to Zeus, we can perhaps assume that this festival
included the sacrifice of a bull. The name Kouretes derives from
*Kouros*, a 'boy' or 'young man'. Hence Jane Harrison's conclusion that the Kouretes symbolize young men who have been
initiated themselves and will initiate others, instructing them in
tribal duties and dances and, having stolen them away from their
mothers, will hide them and make away with them by a pre-
tended death and then will bring them back as new-born, grown
youths, full members of their tribe.

Zeus is invoked in the hymn as son of Kronos, and at the
same time, 'greatest Kouros', that is, as the personification of
the most worthy of themselves by the youthful celebrants. In the
second stanza, the birth of Zeus and the guardianship of the
Kouretes is mentioned, but at the beginning his annual rebirth
as the Diktaian god of youth is invoked by those who have
themselves been reborn as young citizens. We know that
Diktaian Zeus was represented as a beardless god. The hymn
explains the aptness of this conception. The annual return of the
young god coincides with the replenishment of the human
resources of the city and is celebrated as the youthful force
which brings this about. But these human resources are part of
nature and the life of the city is equally dependent on natural
resources which must also be renewed and made to flourish
through the same regenerative force. So, in the later part of the
hymn, there are old, sacred formulae of the magic of fertility.
The young Zeus is invoked to bring about the increase of cattle,
flocks, corn, cities, seafaring ships, the youth of the cities and
the lawful order of those cities. Animals, crops, human beings
and abstract concepts essential to the collective well-being of

the city-state are bound together by the same need of annual renewal brought about by the return of the young god to Dikte through the invocation of those who have emerged into a new life themselves.

The many legends associated with the nurture of the infant Zeus in the cave by bees or doves, or goat or pig are survivals from the earliest totemistic strata of Greek religion which collected about the Hellenic anthropomorphic Zeus and which he never entirely abandoned in popular belief. Thus, for example, the Cretans continued to have a taboo on sow's flesh and Athenaios has preserved the traditional explanation of the taboo.[6] The sanctity of swine among the Cretans was referred to in the myth of the birth of Zeus on Mount Dikte, where a mysterious sacrifice also took place. A sow was thought to have suckled Zeus and made his whimpers inaudible to passers-by by grunting as it trotted round the child. Therefore everybody looked upon the sow as an especially sacred animal and abstained from eating its flesh. Moreover, the people of the city of Praisos actually made offerings to a pig and this was their customary sacrifice before marriage. This latter report is in keeping with other evidence which indicates that the Praisians of eastern Crete preserved their links with the old Minoan stock until late in the historical period.

The Olympian deities were immortal. However, the Cretans not only celebrated the annual reincarnation of a youthful Zeus, but mourned his death. St. Paul and other Christian writers have echoed the strictures of Kallimachos upon the lying Cretans. For the poet was shocked by their belief in a Zeus who died. Nevertheless, legends about the tomb of Zeus have endured from ancient into modern times, with its various locations at Knossos, Mount Ida or Mount Dikte. There are different versions too of an inscription on this tomb. Taken together, they suggest that an old name Zan for Zeus was common in Crete; and that the cult of Zeus may have developed from, or at least have been closely linked with, an earlier cult of Minos. The bond between these strata for long continued to be an annual festival in honour of a fertility god like Adonis and Tammuz, where this god was eaten in the form of a bull. Though the evidence for the tomb of Zeus and its epitaph derive from late antiquity, it firmly

[6] 9.375 f–376 a.

indicates that Cretan-born Zeus was conceived as a god who died annually and was born again.[7]

Now the god Dionysos was also a bull-god, a dying god and a child not reared by his mother. There is general agreement that he is so similar to Cretan-born Zeus that there was small place for his independent worship in Crete. There is no doubt that this assumption is correct, even though the evidence for the worship of Dionysos, especially in the western part of Crete, is rather more extensive than has sometimes been supposed. The explanation seems to be that cults of Dionysos developed in Crete in historical times under the influence of the revival of Orphic mystery cults in the sixth century B.C. on the mainland. Such cults could reinforce, even though they could never supplant, the traditional mystery cults of Crete centred upon the Cretan-born Zeus. This conclusion can be illustrated by a famous fragment from *The Cretans* of Euripides, translated in part here thus:

> Thou lord over Crete with her hundred
> Towns, O thou son of the mighty Zan
> And Europa, Phoenician-born.
>
> Unsullied the life I have led since
> I became initiate of Idaian Zeus
> And herdsman of Zagreus who wanders by night,
> Accomplished the raw-flesh feasts and held high
> Torches to the Mountain-mother, torches
> Of the Kouretes,
> Hallowed and named as a Bakkhos.

Euripides did not think it incongruous to depict the cult of Cretan Zeus in mystical terms when he was writing in the fifth century B.C. The fragment is cited by Porphyrios, who explains that it was delivered by the inspired Cretan worshippers of Zeus who formed the chorus of the play. The Zeus of the fragment is named the Zeus of Ida, but he is honoured by the Kouretes and is essentially the same Zeus of the Hymn of the Kouretes of Palaikastro, and so like Dionysos that the initiated mystics can refer to themselves as his followers, Bakkhoi. The mysteries of this god who dies and is born again, who renews

[7] Detailed evidence cited in Willetts, CCF 219.

life in his worshippers, culminated in the devouring of the raw flesh of the god himself, made manifest in the form of a bull.[8]

There is now much evidence to support the view that this cycle of mythology of a bull-god originated with the Babylonian Hymn of Creation (*Enuma elish*) and that it came to Crete by way of Ugarit in the course of the second millennium B.C. For the idea of regenerative force was personified, for the Canaanites of Ugarit, by a bull and in some documents the god El is Shor-El or the Bull-El. As a bull he is united with the goddess Asherat-of-the-Sea, mother and counsellor of the gods. The third deity of importance after El and Asherat was Baal, the god of heights, storms and rains, sending lightning and carrying a thunderbolt. Baal had a bull's strength, overcame enemies with his horns and had a horned helmet. The head of a bull was his symbol and his priests are sometimes portrayed with animal masks and horns. Baal was accompanied, or at times replaced, by his son Aliyan, the protector of springs and waters, symbol of the growth of plants in the rainy season. This pair ruled through the autumn, winter and spring, to be replaced in the summer by the spirit of harvest, the god Mot, ruler of the dry earth. Mot began to fight with Baal and Aliyan every spring and won his fight in the summer as the fruit ripened. As the rains stopped, Baal vanished. Aliyan survived while there was still water in the springs and river-beds. Then he too had to leave the earth as the hot season advanced. Before he did so, however, he obeyed his father's behest and formed a symbolic union with a heifer, so as to safe-guard the increase of cattle.

The heifer was the goddess Anat, Aliyan's sister, and now his lover. When Aliyan died, Anat searched for him and found his body in the home of the dead inside the earth. She carried the body to the heights of Saphon and buried it with sacrifices of wild bulls, oxen, sheep, deer, wild goats and wild asses. She then appealed to Mot to restore Aliyan. When he refused, she killed him and scattered his flesh in the fields. This sacrifice of Mot was a harvest rite, a form of the well-known ritual of the last sheaf, intended to give back the spirit of vegetation to the fields and so ensure crops in the following year. Mot was already an anthropomorphic god but he was nevertheless, in Ugaritic myth and ritual, cooked and treated like the last sheaf at harvest-

[8] Porph. *Abst.* 4.19; E. *fr.* 472 Nauck; Willetts, CCF 239–41.

time. This underlying ritual attached to other anthropomorphic gods of antiquity such as Osiris, Tammuz, Adonis, Dionysos, Bacchus and the Cretan-born Zeus.

It is the myth of Europa which forms one of the strongest links between Crete and Syria; and it happens that the two Phoenician cities of Tyre and Sidon in Asia Minor and the city of Gortyn in Crete, on the evidence of their coinage in historical times, persistently preserved the story of Europa. In fact, a Byzantine tradition tells us that Gortyn had had four names, the first of them being Hellotis, which was how Europa was called among the Cretans.

In mythology, Belos and Agenor were sons of Poseidon and Libya. Belos became king of Egypt, while Agenor settled in Phoenicia and his children were Europa, Phoenix, Kilix and Kadmos. Disguised as a bull, Zeus brought Europa to Crete and she became the mother of Minos. Kilix and Kadmos searched for their sister, Kadmos travelling to Delphi by way of Rhodes and Thasos. He was told by the oracle at Delphi to abandon his search and follow a cow to a place where it would sit down. This place became the site of Thebes. Herodotos also tells us that Europa came to Crete from Phoenicia.[9] It seems highly probable then that the myth of Zeus and Europa was closely associated with the Phoenician myth of El and Asherat. But the anthropomorphic Zeus who later became the partner of Europa may not have achieved his final evolution from a bull-god until the Mycenaean period. However that may be, it is certain that animal sacrifices continued to be a prominent feature of the ritual of his worship. Rams and, more frequently, oxen were the normal sacrificial animals, both being associated with sky-gods in general and particularly with Zeus. As A. B. Cook pointed out, they were the most precious victims that pastoral peoples could offer, and from their point of view, the most possessed of fertilizing power and consequently the most essential both for their economy and for their survival.

The sacred marriage of Zeus and Europa took place, according to tradition, in or under an evergreen plane-tree near a stream at Gortyn. The archaic Europa, riding on a bull, is depicted on the earliest coins of Gortyn and Phaistos. The pictorial character of these coins has led to the suggestion that

[9] 1. 1–2.

they derived from local frescoes. A famous coin-series from Gortyn portrays the story of the sacred marriage of Zeus and Europa. The goddess at first sits in a willow-tree, while the bull, on the reverse of the coin, licks his flank. Then Zeus has changed to an eagle and is perched on a branch beside Europa, who lifts her veil with the gesture of a bride. On the reverse the bull is teased by a gad-fly. The final scene is the embrace, with Europa and the eagle joined like Leda and the swan.

Europa in art is often portrayed sitting on the bull, holding his fertilizing horn in one hand and in the other hand a flower, magic symbol of her own fertility. For the sacred marriage of Zeus and Europa, as depicted in art, literature and coinage, not only unites Mycenaean and Minoan cult and mythology, but carries traces of belief which must go back to the earliest neolithic phases of habitation. We saw that there was a link in tradition between Europa and Hellotis. This primitive goddess Hellotis had a festival called the Hellotia. We are told that a garland of myrtle, thirty feet in circumference, was carried in procession at this festival and that the bones of Europa, called Hellotis, were carried in the garland. This old goddess with her festival of garland and bones existed before Europa arrived to be joined with her in popular belief, and indeed before there was a god, even a bull-god, to act as dominant partner in a sacred marriage.[10]

For there was no male anthropomorphic divinity in neolithic times. A Cretan male deity is a relatively late religious phenomenon and his role is, to begin with, quite subordinate. A male deity certainly begins to emerge in Minoan times but, in general, Minoan religion was dominated by the worship of the mother-goddess from Middle Minoan times. This dominant anthropomorphic goddess appears with many religious symbols, with animals, birds and snakes, with the sacred tree in a stylized form, with poppies and lilies, with swords and double-axes, with the horns of the bull, so-called horns of consecration. Most of these symbols derived from Anatolia and were presumably part of the customary tribal lore of the early inhabitants.

The standard Minoan burial custom at all periods was collective interment in natural caves, stone chambers and *tholos* tombs.

[10] Cornford, PS 239–49 and note by E. R. Dodds, *ibid.* 249; Barnett, EKTH; Thomson, SAGS 2 140–55; Willetts, CCF 152–68.

All around the great plain of Messara the remains of dense settlements have been found together with large vaulted tombs. The burying of the dead in large communal graves is an indication of social organization based on clans. However, individual interment in stone cists, jars and clay coffins began before the end of Early Minoan times and steadily increased thereafter. This growing practice certainly points to the disintegration of the clan system, but there are various other considerations to be borne in mind. Jar burials may be exceptional. For the custom of burying infants in jars, with the intention of reimpregnating the mother with the spirit of the dead child, is very common. Again, individual interment did not become standard practice. Finally, as we have seen, collective customs based on the *oikos* as a social unit developed out of the clan, exerted a marked influence well into historical times. Of course, the arrival of the Dorians meant a fresh influx of tribal organization and customs superimposed upon the way of life of the old inhabitants. Nevertheless, collective forms of social organization must have independently survived right through the Bronze Age from neolithic times. The part played by tribes, clans and households in Minoan times is unknown and has to be cautiously assessed by analogy and inference in conjunction with archaeological data. There are certain indications, including the evidence from late survivals in the historical period, that the Minoan social organization was matrilineal. There is no denying the high social position of women in Minoan times. Their freedom in domestic and social life is clearly in evidence, they often did men's work, and took part in sports and games, including bull-fighting. A matrilineal social organization could account for the dominating role of the mother-goddess. In such a social system, the women would have played the leading part in maintaining the clan and household cults.

The palaces were the main centres of social development in Minoan times and, in these great households, the goddess grew in stature from her primitive origins, which are indicated in the figurines which have survived from early times and whose Protogeometric and Geometric counterparts continued to exhibit a Minoan tradition. Early Cretan types of human figurine, together with clay birds and animals, were found in the neolithic strata of Knossos. The majority of the human types were female. Analysing their connexions, Evans considered that we have to do with parallel phenomena, whose operation is traceable throughout a continuous region extending from the Aegean, and the Adriatic, to the Persian Gulf and even beyond the Caspian. He also thought that some distant connexion might ultimately be established between this neolithic family and the still earlier images of the Aurignacian Age with the organs of maternity so prominently shown, of which the 'Venus of Brassempouy' and that of Willendorf in Lower Austria stand as classical examples. The figurines common in neolithic and chalcolithic sites from central Europe, the Mediterranean region and the Near East are generically similar to palaeolithic types. They were usually made of clay, less frequently carved in stone, most of them female, though including male statuettes and models of animals. The people who made these figurines had become settled food-producers. The magic rituals of their hunting predecessors can be, at least partly, understood through the interpretation of the mural art of the Upper Palaeolithic hunting culture which survives in certain caves and rock shelters. These rituals appear to have linked together the life and death of animals and human beings in the form of totemic imagery, symbols of ancestry and rebirth. They were transformed into the fertility cults of the settled cultivators.

Nature and society were now conceived as dependent upon the earth, not upon the animals who roamed the earth. The link between them was for a long time imagined as a female principle. The work of agriculture does not pass from women to men until field-tillage and the cattle-drawn plough replace garden-tillage and hoe cultivation; and matrilineal descent tends to continue until this stage is reached. The greater frequency of the female figurine can therefore be correlated both with the ritual role of female labour in the work of agriculture and with the concept of the dominance of the female in the cycle of human reproduction. This changing pattern of magical ritual was presumably woven into the traditions of the neolithic immigrants into Crete. This assumption is supported by the fact that Cretan caves and rock shelters continued to be important centres of cult.

Early Minoan figurines were apparently fashioned under foreign influence, partly Egyptian and partly Cycladic. Cycladic idols imported into Crete were made of Parian marble, for

instance. The many terracotta and bronze types of Middle and
Late Minoan times consist of votive images from sanctuaries,
cult idols from shrines, and others from graves and tombs. They
assume varied attitudes which presumably represent a variety of
functions. The posture of the earliest examples suggests that
adopted in childbirth, and the variety of the later types seems to
indicate their magical efficacy in association with death, which
would account for their presence in graves and tombs, and as
votive offerings to the goddess in supplication for help in sick-
ness or childbirth, or at other crucial times, such as initiation,
marriage or bereavement, and as images of the goddess herself,
meant as gifts in thanks for her patronage.[11]

The caves of Crete have supplied much evidence of their use
as cult centres from neolithic times until the historical period,
and it has been inferred that the cave-cult of Minoan divinities
was the major characteristic of popular religion. In Crete, as
elsewhere, cave-mouths and rock shelters were used for habitation and the practice of burying the dead in such places survived
after people had begun to live in huts and houses. In fact, caves
and rock shelters were used for burials into Late Minoan times.
That many caves were used as shrines is clear from the votive
offerings discovered in them. It is equally clear that, from early
times until the Roman period, caves were associated with religious practices. Though new deities took the place of older ones,
the new cults inherited age-old traditions, and there is much
evidence of continuity in the form of idols, cult objects and
actual buildings, but above all in the cult of such goddesses as
Europa, whose role has been discussed, Demeter, Eileithyia,
Leto, Britomartis and Diktynna, and also in some aspects of the
worship of more typically Olympian deities.

In this respect such goddesses were fulfilling the role played
by the Mother-goddess who dominated Minoan religion and
at the same time perpetuated older beliefs and practices represented by the fetishes and symbols which surrounded her, and
which in turn often reflect the social functions of women. The
figurines typify the variety of these functions in certain directions. Other attributes testify in other ways. Thus, the axe probably owed its sacral associations to its use in cutting timber,

[11] Evans, PM 1.43–55; Nilsson, MMR 290ff.; Thomson, SAGS I².240ff.;
Willetts, CCF 55–9.

which is work done by women in primitive societies. A woman carrying a double-axe is a characteristic feature in the neolithic culture of the Tarn and Garonne; and the Minoan double-axe is never found in the hands of a male god. The principal Minoan domestic cult was that of the snake, in association with the goddess. Because it casts its slough and renews itself, the snake signifies immortality, and snakes are incarnations of the dead. The snake, as a fertility symbol attached to the goddess as protectress of the household, was presumably under the special care of women. Later, the snake-cult became attached to the male deities who succeeded the goddess. Special mention should be made here of Asklepios, the physician-god, whose cult was of special importance in Crete in historical times.

From the evidence of monuments, the nomenclature of later deities and also of mythology, we can conclude that the Minoan goddess was a moon-goddess as well as a fertility-goddess. In fact, the two roles are closely associated. The worship of the moon is connected with the time-keeping systems of early agricultural communities. Sacrificial animals offered by women to the moon normally are small species, in particular, the hare, goat and pig, doves and also cats. The Cretan goddess was certainly associated with goats and doves, and pigs and cats are also represented in various Minoan contexts. The moon is also looked upon, in primitive communities, as a stimulus to fertility in plants and vegetation. The social tasks of women in such communities include the tending of plants, just as herbal magic is their special care. For plants, flowers and seeds were used in menstruation, pregnancy and childbirth. Even in the time of Pliny, the lily was considered a check to menstruation; and the poppy was looked upon for a long time in antiquity as symbolizing fecundity. We can understand then why the lily was a specially sacred Minoan flower. Ritual dances in a field of lilies take place before the goddess. When she is throned, a lily appears at her feet. Female attendants offer a bunch of lilies. Poppy capsules are sometimes offered instead.[12]

Much of this lore was passed on to the goddesses whom we can definitely name, unlike the Mother-goddess who, though nameless, had so many functions.

Demeter is said to have reached Greece from Crete and

[12] Evans, PM 2.776–7, 3.458; Persson, RGPT 74–5.

Homer tells of the sacred marriage of Demeter and Iasion in Crete.[13] The sacred marriage is bound up with the religious concept of the vegetation cycle, the death and rebirth of crops. The Cretan Demeter had much in common with Oriental rituals such as those of Magna Mater and Atthis, Ishtar and Tammuz, Aphrodite and Adonis. She supplied Triptolemos with seed-corn and a plough and sent him over the world to teach the art of agriculture to mankind. The myth of Demeter and Persephone reminds us of the double aspect of the Minoan goddess as Mother and Maid; and Demeter's attributes of snakes, trees, poppies and small animals show that she was an emanation of that goddess.

The Eleusinian Mysteries were performed in honour of Demeter and Persephone. These mysteries, according to the Homeric Hymn to Demeter, and to Diodoros, were brought to Greece from Crete. Diodoros wrote:[14] 'As what they consider to be the chief proof of their contention that divine honours, sacrifices and rites involved in the Mysteries were transmitted from Crete to other peoples, the Cretans advance the following argument. The rite celebrated by the Athenians at Eleusis, perhaps the most remarkable of all, the one in Samothraike, and that in Thrace among the Kikones, whence came Orpheus who introduced them—these were all transmitted in secret forms. At Knossos in Crete, however, it was customary, from ancient times, for these rites to be transmitted to all quite openly; and such things as are elsewhere transmitted in secret are there not concealed from anyone who wishes to know about them. They declare that most of the gods proceeded from Crete to many parts of the inhabited world, conferring benefits upon the races of men and sharing among each of them the advantages of their own discoveries. Thus Demeter passed over into Attica and from there to Sicily and, later on, to Egypt. In these places especially she received great honours among those she benefited in transmitting the fruit of the corn and in teaching them about the sowing of the seed.'

Eileithyia was a goddess of childbirth. Homer tells how she attended Leto when Apollo was born in Delos. The cave of Eileithyia at Amnisos, ancient harbour of Knossos, is also mentioned by Homer and this Homeric tradition must go back to

[13] *Od.* 5.125–8.       [14] 5.77.3–5.

Minoan times. The cave has been explored and revealed evidence of continuity of a cult from neolithic times and of a revival in the Roman period. The name of the goddess is not Indo-European and this confirms the likelihood of her direct descent from the Minoan goddess.[15]

The cult of Leto (Doric Lato) and her son Apollo originated in Asia Minor but their association with Crete has long been considered to be important, if only because the cult of the goddess was more prominent in Crete as compared with Greece itself. The evidence for this survival is concentrated in central and eastern Crete. We have already noticed the connexion between Lato and the district of Gortyn known as Latosion. But it is her festival at Phaistos which is of special value in establishing Lato's connexion with Minoan and even earlier cults. This festival was known as the Ekdysia, during which the youths put aside their boyish garments and assumed men's clothes. It was connected with the cult of Lato Phytia, Lato 'the productive'. Phytia, like Physkoa at Olympia and perhaps Orthia at Sparta, was a goddess promoting growth, including growth of fertility in the youth of the city, now to be initiated at the annual festival into manhood, citizenship and marriage after leaving the 'herd'. I have elsewhere maintained that Lato Phytia and her festival were rooted in the earliest stratum of Cretan religion.[16] There is some indication that the festival at one time included, if it was not restricted to, girl initiates. Their later exclusion was part of a process whereby the ritual of the sacred marriage grew out of primitive collective union, whereby also coronation became a special form of initiation following upon a pre-nuptial ordeal. The name Lato has been connected with the Carian word *lada*, meaning 'woman'. Minoans and Carians had been closely related in the Bronze Age according to tradition and as archaeology increasingly confirms. A Carian cult of the 'Woman' would have been very similar to the Minoan cult of the Mother-goddess and the similarity may account for the borrowing of the name.

Britomartis and Diktynna were somehow closely related and the evidence about their cults perhaps indicates that this relationship is that of Mother and Maid, that Diktynna is to Demeter as Britomartis to Persephone. Britomartis is a Minoan name which

---

[15] *Od.* 19.188, *H.Ap.* 115–22; Nilsson, MMR 58.       [16] CCF 176ff.

means 'sweet maiden'. She was connected with Minos in mythology. For she was said to have escaped his pursuit by disappearing into a grove at Aigina, where she was worshipped as Aphaia. Or she was said to have been the companion of Artemis, and, pursued by Minos for nine months, threw herself into the sea to make her escape. Britomartis might have become wholly assimilated by Artemis, if her cult had not been tenaciously preserved in a number of places, as for example at Dreros, where she is distinguished from Artemis in the Drerian oath. The epigraphic evidence in general seems to show that her worship lasted from early times in central Crete and especially along the north coast.[17]

In prehistoric times there were Carian settlements far beyond the bounds of Caria itself, not only along the Asiatic coast but in the Cyclades and on the mainland of Greece. Thucydides tells us that Minos ruled over the Cyclades and expelled the Carians. Cretan tradition, as reported by Herodotos, said that the Carians came into the mainland from the islands; that they manned the ships of Minos and, since Minos subdued an extensive area, the Carians were the most renowned of peoples in those days.[18]

The widespread cult of Diktynna lies within the bounds of the old Carian domain and was therefore perhaps part of a religious complex which includes, but cannot be localized in Crete, although the Cretan name was etymologically connected with Mount Dikte. Indeed, the Diktynna represented on coins as late as Trajan's time still bears her primitive aspect of mountain mother, guardian of initiates, maid become mother, Britomartis mature.

A principal centre of her worship was at a temple on the northwest coast, the Diktynnaion, on the promontory between Phalasarna and Kydonia. The Diktynnaion was under the control of the Kydonians for long periods in historical times, but after the Roman occupation control passed, not for the first time, to the Polyrhenians. We know from the epigraphic evidence that, in the times of Hadrian and other emperors, the revenues of the temple belonged to the public treasury and were used to finance public works, including roads, throughout the Province of Crete.

The city of Aptera lay not far to the east of Kydonia. In the

[17] *Ibid.* 180.　　　　　[18] Thuc. 1.4; Hdt. 1.171.

calendar of this city there was a month named after Diktynna (Diktynnaios) in Hellenistic times. Here too there was an important temple of Artemis, where she was worshipped as Aptera, 'Wingless Artemis'. This 'Wingless Artemis' was, like Diktynna, a protectress of youth, close to her Minoan proto-type. The mythology associated with her worship, together with recent archaeological investigation, indicates that her cult was originally based upon a rite of initiation and purification per-formed, not by young men, but by female initiates.

According to mythology, a contest took place at Aptera between the Sirens and the Muses, in which the Muses were victorious. They plucked out the feathers of the Sirens who then became white and threw themselves into the sea. The town was consequently called Aptera and some neighbouring islands Leukai ('white'). A contest between rival choirs of females thus ended with a ritual ordeal of a leap into the sea. The leap into the sea is a feature of Minoan religion based on initiation myths. The example of Britomartis who leapt into the sea to escape from Minos is one of several which could be cited.

The caves of Crete have recently been carefully surveyed by the French archaeologist, P. Faure.[19] His survey of the penin-sula of Akrotiri, north-east of Khania (ancient Kydonia), led him to conclude that the whole area was thickly populated by the end of the Bronze Age. Ancient tradition held that Zeus was here suckled by a bitch, who was metamorphosed into a bear. Coins of the Roman Imperial period represent Diktynna holding the young Zeus; and at Kydonia, as in other places in western Crete, Diktynna is associated with Cretan-born Zeus.

In a cave on Akrotiri called Arkoudia ('Cave of the She-Bear') were discovered several heads of Artemis, of Classical and Hellenistic times. The local myth, as Faure has argued, points to a ritual concerned with a sacred bear and a goddess, guardian of the young, worshipped by pre-Dorian inhabitants. The cave is nowadays consecrated to the Purification of the Virgin, known locally as Panagia Arkoudiotissa, and with an annual festival. A cult of the Mother has therefore been located here at least from Minoan times. The great central stalagmite in the cave, in the shape of a bear (or a bitch), Faure would link with the local ancient myth of the birth and childhood of Zeus.

[19] Faure, FCC.

The Bear-goddess Artemis is no novelty. Arkas, who gave his name to Arcadia, was changed into a bear before he was born. The mother was named Kallisto, Megisto or Themisto, all epithets of Artemis. The town of Kyzikos, on the Propontis, was built on a hill called the Bear Mountain and the nurses of Zeus were traditionally bears. Above all, at Brauron, in Attica, where some recent archaeological investigation has thrown further light on the cult, Artemis Brauronia had a temple. Here girl initiates, dressed in saffron, performed a bear-dance before they were married.

Artemis and Diktynna maintained close links with each other therefore and, throughout historical times in antiquity, also showed clear traces of their original descent from the Minoan Mother-goddess. In the same way, Aphrodite Skotia at Phaistos, as we saw, continued to be regarded as the special patron of young men who were to be initiated into manhood and marriage. One of the epithets of Athene in Crete was Wadia ('Sweet'). This name occurs also in Elis, on the mainland, where there was a cult of 'Athene the Mother'. In Crete then, as in Elis, Athene could still be regarded as a fertility-goddess, Mother and Maid, like the Minoan goddess, linked to Britomartis, another 'Sweet Maid'.

The Olympian goddesses also sometimes thus perpetuated the cults inherited from the Minoan goddess, no less than the goddesses who can be regarded as more specifically Cretan. Zeus too, father of the Olympians, though he had more than a score of epithets in Classical and Hellenistic times, was dominant as the Cretan Zeus, the fertility god who died and was annually reborn. The cult and mythology of the youthful Cretan Zeus are constant reminders that, though the Olympian gods were pre-eminent in conventional Hellenic religion, there was a time when the reverse had been the case, when the Mother-goddess had been all-important and the male a late and subordinate element. The stature of the male god, son or consort of the Mother-goddess, does, however, increase in later Minoan times. This growth in stature must have coincided with changes in the social status of men, with modifications in the old system of communal relations and of matrilineal rights. In religious terms, the element of continuity in the fertility cycle was featured in the goddess, maintainer of life in nature and in human beings, while the element of discontinuity, symbol of the pattern of birth, death and renewal, was the god. He shared the mortality of the seed, gathered at the harvest and returned to the earth, and hence was a dying god, dying as the son or lover of the goddess. At Knossos, this god was apparently conceived as a bull-god. This conception may underlie the myth of the Minotaur, loved by Queen Pasiphae, wife of Minos; and the ritual behind the myth could have been a form of the sacred marriage, with the priest-king acting the male part, masked in the head of a bull. Furthermore, since the sun was conceived as a bull, it has been suggested that the Labyrinth at Knossos was an arena of solar pattern where a mimetic dance was performed by a dancer dressed as a bull and representing the movements of the sun.[20]

Although evidence from the monuments is scanty, Evans correctly described the King of Knossos as a 'priest-king', analogous to Oriental priest-kings who represented a god, wore his dress, exerted his authority and often were called by his name. Hence the presumption that the 'Room of the Throne' at Knossos was used for rites of initiation and purification, presided over by the Minoan priest-king, as the adopted son on earth of the Cretan Mother-goddess.[21]

At this point we must add something further to what was said earlier (pp. 42f.) about the priest-king and the calendar. Homer describes Minos as a nine-year king, familiar of Zeus. Plato and others record the tradition that Minos retired every ninth year to the cave of Zeus and renewed his familiar intercourse with the god. Since Zeus is a later intruder, these legends indicate that the Minoan priest-king was a young man whose tenure of office was dependent upon the periodically renewed sanction of the Minoan Mother-goddess, for whom Zeus, the male deity, was substituted in the Homeric and the later Greek tradition. The nine-year intervals of renewal were really eight-year intervals, because, in reckoning intervals of time, the Greeks included both the terms separated by the interval. There is much evidence from literary, mythological and archaeological sources, of a close connexion between this octennium, as it is called, and the ancient kingship of the Bronze Age. In ancient Greece the year was divided into twelve months alternating between twenty-

[20] Frazer, GB 3.71; Cook Z.1.521ff.
[21] Evans, PM 1.1–7; Nilsson, MMR 486.

nine and thirty days. The deficit of eleven days was made good by intercalating a thirteenth month in three years out of every eight. Professor George Thomson has brought forward much evidence to support the view that this lunisolar calendar, based on the octennial cycle, goes back to the Minoan Age. The 'priest-king's' duties would thus have included regulation of the calendar and his period of tenure of office would have been closely bound up with the ritual of time-reckoning, essential for an agricultural community, where sun and bull had become combined in cult and both were attached to the kingship.[22]

[22] H. *Od.* 19.178–9, sch. *ad loc*; Pl. *Min.* 319 c, *Lg.* 624 d; Str. 10.476; D.S. 5.78.3; Max. Tyr. 38.2; Val. Max. 1.2. ext. 1; *EM* s.v. ἐννέωροι; Frazer, GB 3.58–92; Thomson, SAGS 2 127–30; Willetts, CCF 92–103.

# XI

❖◇◇◇◇◇◇◇◇◇◇◇◇◇◇◇◇◇◇◇◇◇◇◇◇◇◇◇◇◇◇◇◇◇◇◇◇◇◇◇◇◇❖

## Pirates and Mercenaries

❖◇◇◇◇◇◇◇◇◇◇◇◇◇◇◇◇◇◇◇◇◇◇◇◇◇◇◇◇◇◇◇◇◇◇◇◇◇◇◇◇◇❖

Piracy has been a constant activity of the sea-going peoples of the Aegean from remote antiquity until recent times. Even at the end of the eighteenth century it was an Aegean custom for the proceeds of a voyage, whether commercial or piratical, to be halved, one part passing to the shareholders of the ship, the other equally divided among the crew.

When Thucydides mentions the tradition that Minos established a navy, made himself the master of the greater part of the Hellenic sea and ruled over the Cyclades, he adds that Minos also did his best to suppress piracy so as to secure a ready supply of revenues for himself. From early times, Thucydides then explains, both Greeks and barbarians from the coastal areas and the islands turned to piracy as sea-communications developed, under the stimulus of personal greed and to support the needy. These pirates would attack and plunder towns which were really clusters of villages because they lacked the protection of walls. No disgrace attached to what became a principal source of livelihood but, on the contrary, some measure of renown. So much was clear from the esteem which a successful pirate could still gain among mainland people in his own day and from the common habit, reported by the old poets, of asking voyagers if they were pirates, in a way which shows that those who were questioned would not have refuted a suggestion which in turn implied no reproach.

140

The historian makes clear that the prevalence of piracy in early times and its temporary suppression by Minos naturally affected the siting of towns. For older cities, both on the islands and on the mainland, were built more at a distance from the sea, since pirates not only plundered one another but also those coastal dwellers who were not sea-faring people. The same practice of building cities away from the coast was common in his own day, he says. Indeed, as Hasebroek has pointed out, piracy and privateering were practised with the protection and authority of the state, and in all periods of Greek history were recognized professions and lawful institutions; so much so that in Athenian law companies of privateers were treated like any other form of association and Greek treaties often included agreements about piratical rights.[1]

However, from the time of Minos onward, maritime powers were able to suppress piracy in varying degrees and for varying periods. Here Thucydides acknowledged that the cities founded in more recent times, when navigation became safer, were built on the coast, and fortified cities were established on peninsulas, connected with the mainland by an isthmus.

This account of Thucydides is confirmed by investigation of settlement sites in Crete. Occupied areas were removed from the coastal plains to higher levels at times when piracy was unchecked. Minoan settlements were often not very high above sea level, but in post-Minoan times, the villagers settled on higher ground. When Pompey had suppressed the pirates in the first century B.C., the plains on the coast were again occupied by the inhabitants. There was a further withdrawal in the times of the Saracen marauders in the early ninth century and a subsequent return to the coasts under Venetian rule.

Piracy and brigandage were normal activities of the Homeric heroes. When he returns to Ithaca, Odysseus does not reveal his identity until he is ready to take his revenge on the suitors. He tells a false tale about himself and his background, and what he has to say gives us some idea of the actual state of affairs in post-Minoan Crete. There is clearly no firm political authority, conditions generally are unsettled and sea-raiding is a common enterprise.

Odysseus tells his swineherd Eumaios that he is a Cretan, son

[1] Thuc. 1.4ff.; Hasebroek, TPAG 118 *et passim*; Hutchinson, PC 35-6.

of a rich man and a concubine, but put on an equal footing, by his father, with his legitimate sons. When his father died, his sons divided his estate by lot but gave only a meagre share to the illegitimate son. However, he was able to marry into a wealthy family on the strength of his natural gifts of courage and good sense. He had never feared death in battle but had always leaped to the fight before anyone else when he had picked his men for an ambush.

'That is how I was in a battle,' he goes on. 'But I had no taste for work nor for those homely enterprises that foster a fine family. No, ships with oars were always my pleasure, and battles and well-polished javelins and arrows, baneful things, which make other people shudder. I suppose such things delighted my spirit because heaven made me that way. For one kind of work pleases some people, others like another. So, before the Achaeans ever went to Troy, I had commanded my own swift ships and men against peoples overseas as a result of which much booty came my way. From this I would choose what suited my taste and get much else besides from what was divided out among us. My household goods quickly multiplied and I became both feared and respected among the Cretans.'

Then came the Trojan War. He and Idomeneus were persuaded to undertake command of the Cretan contingent. The Greeks took Priam's city in the tenth year of the war and sailed for home. After a single month spent in the pleasures of home life with his wife, his children and his possessions, he gave in to the temptation to equip a fleet and sail for Egypt. Nine ships were made ready and their crews quickly mustered. After a week spent in festivity, they sailed away from Crete and arrived without mishap in the Nile. He ordered the crews to stay at the ships and sent out a reconnaissance party. But these men gave way to violence and suddenly started to ravage some of the fine Egyptian farms, killing the men and carrying off women and children. An alarm was soon raised in the city and the Cretan force was overrun, many being killed and the rest enslaved, but for their commander, who saved himself by surrendering to the king of the Egyptian troops. The king spared his life and saved him from the wrath of his followers.

He stayed on in Egypt for seven years and acquired much wealth from the Egyptians who treated him well. Then he made the acquaintance of a rogue, a grasping Phoenician, who persuaded him to travel home with him to Phoenicia where he spent a year on this man's estate. The Phoenician then took him on board a ship bound for Libya on the excuse that he needed his help with the cargo, but really intending to sell him for a large sum of money at the journey's end. However, the ship was wrecked in a storm. The Cretan was the only survivor and was cast up on the coast of Thesprotia. The king of the Thesprotians gave him hospitality and later sent him on his way on a ship bound for Doulikhion, instructing the crew to treat him well and take him to the king of Doulikhion. Once at sea, however, the crew resolved to enslave their passenger, stripped him of his cloak and tunic and dressed him in a ragged set of clothes. Arriving at the island of Ithaca, they tied up their prisoner and disembarked themselves to take a hasty evening meal on shore. But the Cretan was able to escape from his bonds, swim ashore and hide himself until his captors tired of the search for him.

This tale of vicissitudes, of recurrent good fortune and hard times, of fighting and robbery, of boundless generosity from some and boundless deceit from others, must have been, in some degree, typical of many a real Cretan adventurer in subsequent times whenever piracy was not temporarily suppressed.[2]

Increasing instability at home and a general instability overseas no doubt contributed to the increase of Cretan piracy in Hellenistic times. The Hellenistic period spans the three centuries from Alexander's death in 323 B.C. to the establishment of the Roman Empire by Augustus in 30 B.C. When Alexander died, there was a struggle for power among his generals. Three separate dynasties were consolidated by 275 B.C., descended from three of the generals. A great part of the former Persian empire in Asia came under the Seleucids, Egypt was ruled by the Ptolemies and Macedonia by the Antigonids. The Romans were increasingly active in the affairs of the Hellenistic world after 212 B.C., until they succeeded, through war and diplomacy, in establishing their imperial rule over the Mediterranean world.

Etruscan and other Italian pirates lost their dominance in the early years of the third century B.C. and the Cretans began to be the principal marauders. We find pirates from Allaria in Western Crete being mentioned round about 260 B.C. The

2 *Od.* 13.199–359.

pirates of mainland Aetolia were on friendly terms with the Cretans and they made use of Cretan harbours to assemble their ships and to dispose of their captives. There was a joint raiding expedition against Attica by Aetolians and Cretans and this threat prompted Athens to send ambassadors to a number of Cretan cities to put themselves on a more friendly footing; in 229 B.C. Eumaridas of Kydonia helped the Athenians in their negotiations and the Athenian citizens who had been seized and taken to Crete were ransomed for a sum of twenty talents. We can conclude that the increase in chattel slavery throughout the Mediterranean world in these times was a further stimulus to Cretan piracy. As the raid on Attica and its sequel show, kidnapping was a profitable business. If the victims were not ransomed, they could be sold into slavery. For not only Attica but the islands too were subjected to the raids of Aetolian and Cretan pirates in the course of the third century B.C.

Moreover, from the end of the third century onward, the principal states in time of war made use of pirate forces in a systematic way.[3] Even neutral cities were sometimes raided by such forces. Large-scale raiding and kidnapping continued until the beginning of the second century. In the course of the next half-century, there was a marked decline in Cretan piracy, largely due to the efficiency of the counter-measures adopted by Rhodes. The supply of slaves from Crete began to be so much restricted that other sources of supply were developed by the slave-dealers of Syria, Phoenicia and Asia Minor. Though such negative evidence should not be overmuch relied upon, it may be that the scanty remains of Cretan coinage at this time are associated with the diminution of piracy and a consequent, though temporary, commercial impoverishment. However, the subsequent period of successful Cilician piracy encouraged the revival of piracy in Crete and a return of commercial prosperity, now reflected in an abundance of coinage. For the Cilicians and Cretans seem to have been associated in this period of Cilician piratical supremacy which was eventually terminated by the efforts of the Romans.

The efforts exerted by the Rhodians against the Cretan pirates were prolonged and not always successful. Thus Philip

[3] See Ormerod, PAW *passim*; Rostovtzeff, SEHHW 199, 201–4, 222–3, 607–10, 781–6, 1516–17; Willetts, ASAC 244–5.

of Macedon was able to sabotage their designs by instigating conflict between Rhodes and the Cretans in the so-called Cretan War of 205/4–201 B.C. There was no unity on the Cretan side apparently, and only individual cities carried out raiding expeditions. Rhodes was, however, able to gain the neutrality or friendship of some of the formally hostile Cretan cities by diplomatic means, illustrated, for example, in a surviving treaty with Hierapytna, concluded sometime between 200 and 197 B.C.[4] The Spartan tyrant Nabis continued to avail himself of the services of Cretan pirates and the Rhodian policy of forming alliances with Cretan cities was frustrated during the Third Macedonian War (171–168 B.C.). Cretan cities were engaged on both sides in this war, and since both sides used pirates, Cretan piracy was temporarily stimulated afresh. In 168 B.C. the Rhodians made another determined diplomatic approach, this time to 'all the Cretans', as Polybios informs us, as well as to each individual state.[5] But the Cretans were so determined to maintain their freedom of action as privateers that their city-states arranged to form a united front against Rhodes and her ally Attalus II in the war of 155–153 B.C. Siphnos was actually plundered by the Cretans and their raids were so generally successful that Rhodes was obliged to appeal for help to the Achaean League. The request was refused and the war was brought to an end perhaps through the diplomatic efforts of Rome.

As Beloch observed, between 431 and 346 B.C. there were only thirty-two years when Greece was not the scene of major war. At the end of this period of time, the hired professional mercenary soldier had become a common type. Cretan mercenaries became as familiar as Cretan pirates, especially during the course of the Hellenistic period, when they found employment with Egypt, Syria, Sparta, the Achaean League, Pergamon, Macedonia, Syracuse and Rome. Even before this period Cretan archers had been hired for service in the fifth century B.C. and had been employed too, in Alexander's army. But in Hellenistic times their employment was much more widespread and sometimes they are reported in relatively considerable numbers. For example, in the year 219 B.C., the army of Philip contained a force of 500 Cretans supplied by the Polyrhenians, while Knossos

[4] *Inscr. Cret.* 3.II.3 A.        [5] 29.10.6.

had despatched twice that number of men to support the Aetolians, 500 of them forming a mercenary contingent. A force of 300 Cretans is reported early in the war of Philip against Rome which ended in 197 B.C., at which time the garrison at Corinth included 800 Cretans. When Perseus reviewed his forces at the beginning of the Third Macedonian War in 171 B.C., they included 3,000 Cretans who were under the command of Sosos of Phalasarna and Syllos of Knossos. During the Chremonidean War between the coalition of Athens, Sparta and Ptolemy against Antigonos of Macedonia (267/6–261 B.C.) we hear of 1,000 Cretans serving with the Spartans. In the war of the Allies (220–217 B.C.) the Spartan force included at least 200 Cretans, while King Nabis had a contingent of 2,000 Cretans in his army which opposed Flamininus in 195 B.C. Three years later, the army of the Achaean League, which was campaigning against Nabis, included 500 Cretans. A mercenary force in Alexandria in 221 B.C. contained 1,000 Cretans and in the Egyptian army at the battle of Raphia in 217 B.C. there were no less than 3,000, while in the opposing army of Antiochos III were a further 2,500 Cretans who may have been mercenaries. A force of 1,000 was recruited by Ptolemy Philometor in 163 B.C.

We know that Cretans were serving with Antiochos at the battle of Magnesia in 189 B.C., and that the Pergamene contingent in the Roman army contained 500 Cretan archers. A Cretan force was at Syracuse in 213 B.C. and this may have been made up of the 500 Cretan archers included in the reinforcements despatched by Hieron of Syracuse five years earlier in response to an appeal by the Romans.

This bare statistical record shows how Crete became a source for the recruitment of mercenary forces in the armies of the warring powers of the Mediterranean world. The isolation of Crete was broken indeed. The cities of Crete were increasingly brought into conflict with each other; and, ironically enough, the Cretan mercenaries who might escape from domestic embroilment could find themselves engaged in a kind of artificial internecine struggle by enlistment on opposing sides in a major war abroad. Recruiting campaigns were regularly conducted in the cities of the island in Hellenistic times and the representatives of foreign states appear to have sought permission for such campaigns from the governments of individual Cretan states.

The evidence suggests that the Cretan mercenaries were normally, perhaps exclusively, citizens who could provide their own arms.[6]

Though domestic political considerations no doubt sometimes influenced the city governments when requested to provide mercenaries, they cannot have been normally dominant, to judge from the report of an interview between the Roman Senate and some Cretan ambassadors, in the course of which it was mentioned that there were as many Cretans serving as mercenaries with the armies of Perseus as with those of Rome.[7] Since negotiations for recruiting mercenaries had to be managed by the governments of the city-states, an additional motive was introduced, if it were indeed required, for the oligarchic leaders to intensify their control over the training of the young men who would become citizen soldiers and, therefore, in prevailing conditions, potential mercenaries for foreign powers. Now that such forces were increasingly in demand, the political power of governments was enhanced in so far as they controlled, and could therefore bargain with, an exportable asset of considerable value.

It was fortunate for the oligarchic rulers that piracy and mercenary service could drain off their surplus manpower. There is no evidence that the citizen population of Crete markedly declined in the Hellenistic period. In Sparta, on the other hand, from the beginning of the fifth century B.C. until the third, there was a definite decline in the citizen population. Aristotle considered that Sparta's decline was due to the diminishing number of her citizens, coupled with the weaknesses of the system of land tenure. In his time, as he points out,[8] two-fifths of the land was owned by women and it had fallen into a few hands.

In Crete, too, ownership of the estates had markedly changed in character but in a different way. The tendency already initiated in the Gortyn Code, by the provision relating to division of property, reached its logical conclusion by the time of Polybios, when citizens could have as much land as they were able to acquire. As in Sparta, landed estates were owned by

[6] See further Griffith, MHW *passim*; Parke, GMS *passim*; Tarn and Griffith, HC 92-3, 202; Rostovtzeff, SEHHW 149, 666, 922, 1397, 1516; Van Effenterre, CMG Ch. 6 *et passim*; Willetts, ASAC 246-8.

[7] Liv. 43.7.1ff.; cf. Van Effenterre, CMG 184-94.    [8] *Pol.* 1270 a 11-12.

fewer and fewer people. But the state organization of the food supplies through the *syssitia* meant that poor, as well as richer, citizens had guaranteed for themselves, their wives and children, a constant supply of the necessities of life. More and more citizens owned little or no land but they were not excluded from the *syssitia*, still remained citizens and therefore enjoyed the benefits of the system of food supply which had been praised by Aristotle. That system still depended, as it had for centuries past, upon the subjected serf class.

The young men must have been deprived increasingly of land, therefore. On the other hand they were still trained from boyhood almost entirely in athletic and military pursuits. There was constant warfare between the cities of Crete from the end of the fourth century B.C. until the Roman occupation. Hence their military training was not wasted. Even so, serious discontent must surely have arisen if there had been no other outlet for their energies than to fight in a local war or to wait for the outbreak of another. The Cretan soldier was remarkably well-trained in such types of warfare as ambushes, raids, surprise attacks and night fighting. He was probably not fitted for much else, when he could no longer own and manage land. He certainly had no common cause with the serfs. On the contrary, his whole existence depended on the system of serfdom. Political change of any kind must have seemed dangerous—to the young and to the old. Without piracy and mercenary service, however, demands for a redivision of the land and other radical changes might have found more favourable hearing and more solid support.

# XII

◇◆◇◆◇◆◇◆◇◆◇◆◇◆◇◆◇◆◇◆◇◆◇◆◇◆◇◆◇◆◇◆◇

## Political History

◇◆◇◆◇◆◇◆◇◆◇◆◇◆◇◆◇◆◇◆◇◆◇◆◇◆◇◆◇◆◇◆◇

As we recall the great historical events in which the Greeks of the Classical and Hellenistic ages were so intensely involved— the struggle against the Persian invaders, the no less vital struggle of large masses of citizens for political emancipation within the framework of democratic institutions, the ruinous conflict of the Peloponnesian War, the rise of Macedon and the conquests of Alexander, the subsequent rivalry and warfare between major powers—then, in contrast, the political history of Crete under the Dorian aristocracies may appear to be of slight consequence. Yet, if we remain content with the judgement that the Crete of those times was an insignificant area, overshadowed by the greatness of its own dim past and by its relative isolation from the explosive centres of contemporary historical events, little more than a troublesome nest of pirates or a useful reservoir of mercenary archers and slingers for more dominant powers, we lose the opportunity of gaining fresh insight into some basic contradictory features of the autonomous city-state of ancient Greece.

War and slavery were essential conditions for the existence of the city-state. The freedom of the citizen in a democratic state like Athens depended upon the subjection of the chattel slave. The freedom of the citizen in the aristocratic cities of Crete depended upon the subjection of peasant serfs. The peasantry of Attica played an essential part in the democratic movement. For the peasant class of small-holders became allied with other decisive sections of the population, including the merchants and artisans, in an expanding money economy based on the tenets of private ownership, against the old aristocratic system based on the traditions of landed wealth and narrow privilege. In the early, dynamic phases of democratic innovation, after the reforms of Kleisthenes, ownership became the necessary basis of freedom. In conditions of small-scale production, the free ownership of the self-employed peasant proprietor marked a fresh stage in the development of agriculture as well as being the most suitable form of landed property. The peasant owners of land could advance agricultural production just as the individual free artisan could develop handicraft production, with markedly increased divisions of labour, and a consequent proliferation of social types.

The peasantry of Crete were never, so far as we know, provoked to organized resistance or revolt. They remained in a bondage to the soil and to a landlord system which had been their condition for centuries, perhaps long before the arrival of the Dorians. Small-scale ownership never developed, the serfs remained as instruments of production supporting a minority of landed proprietors.

Although Plato in the *Laws* was not writing as a historian, nevertheless his picture of Crete is sometimes close enough to historical fact to suggest that he had access to accurate information about the social conditions of the island. For instance, the opinion is expressed that Cretan customs are adapted for war, with civic organization more like an army than a city, the young people being herded together like colts at grass. Nevertheless, although war between the states may be endemic, there is no reference to internal strife or to major difficulties between the free and the unfree. In fact when Plato does notice the places where the *syssitia* system has provoked conflict or (what is for him Greece's most serious problem) the Spartan helot-system and similar kinds of bondage, he makes no mention of Crete.[1]

More specifically, when Aristotle introduces his survey of the Spartan constitution, he takes it as axiomatic that good government must be associated with leisure from menial occupations,

[1] Pl. *Lg*. 625e cf. 636b, 666e, 776c–d; Van Effenterre, CMG 74.

though he admits the difficulty of discovering how this leisure is to be guaranteed. The serf class of Thessaly, he goes on, rose against the Thessalians time after time, just like the helots of Sparta, who are like an enemy sitting in wait for misfortunes to fall upon the Spartans. Nothing of this kind, however, he points out, has so far occurred in Crete. A possible reason, he suggests, is that neighbouring cities, even when they are at war with each other, never seek to ally themselves with rebellious elements. For, since they themselves have a serf class, such action would not serve their interests. The Spartans were entirely surrounded, he points out, by hostile neighbours, Argives, Messenians, Arcadians, without such scruples. In the same way, revolts of the serfs against the Thessalians began when they were at war with their neighbours, the Achaeans, and others. Other drawbacks apart, the sheer necessity of controlling a serf class is troublesome and the whole problem of relations with them is beset with difficulties. When they are given some freedom they become insolent and claim the same rights as their masters; if their lives are made miserable they loathe and conspire against them. When a serf-system works out in this way, it is obvious that the best means of handling the problem has not been found. Hence, as we have seen, Aristotle's own ideal solution was that those who tilled the soil should be slaves rather than serfs, to ensure that they were well adapted to labour and safe from the possibility of revolution. The next best arrangement was that they should be foreign serfs of a slave-like temperament. Crete did not, it is true, provide Aristotle with an ideal prototype of a servile peasantry, but it certainly offered him a working example of a practical solution.[2]

The condition of the peasantry of Attica had, before the onset of the democratic movement, roughly corresponded with that of the Cretan serfs except in one major respect. The Attic peasantry were kinsmen not only of the aristocracy who upheld the old economic and political system and to whom they were naturally opposed, but also of those other social classes who were, from different motives, equally desirous of radical change. Alliance of these sections with a rebellious peasantry was therefore dictated by common interests and rendered possible by historical conditions. Peasant liberation was a restoration of ancient rights

[2] Arist. *Pol.* 1269a 29–b 12; cf. p. 64.

in new conditions, thoroughly acceptable as a programme to their allies among other social classes.

Such a development was impossible in Crete. As Aristotle saw, the governing classes of the Cretan states, even when at war, dared not foment rebellion among the serfs of their enemies, in case their own serfs should take the lesson to heart. That Aristotle's judgement of the situation continued to be valid is demonstrated by the evidence of the Itanian oath of the third century B.C. This document clearly indicates that Crete was not immune from the social unrest which had already appeared elsewhere in the Greek world in the previous century. The programme of this movement of social revolution centred upon four major demands: abolition of debt, division of land, confiscation of personal property and liberation of slaves. All the basic features of this programme had apparently been taken over by rebellious sections of the citizens of Itanos—except for the fourth. There is no mention of the liberation of the servile population.[3]

Thus there could be no common ground in formulating demands for radical change between the serfs and other classes. The system endured and was modified, as we have seen, only to the extent of widening the basis of aristocratic rule. When, as Aristotle put it, Crete had been invaded by warfare from abroad, the energies of the younger men were increasingly absorbed in piracy, mercenary service and that almost perpetual warfare between their cities which, apart from enduring servitude and minor constitutional change, largely makes up the dismal chronicle of Cretan political history from the end of the fourth century until the subjugation of the island by the Romans.

The recorded chronicle of rivalry, diplomatic manoeuvre and open warfare begins in 343 B.C. with the capture of Lyttos by Knossos, with the aid of the Phocian mercenary called Phalaikos, and the subsequent defeat of his troops when the Spartan Archidamos came to the rescue of Lyttos. In the course of the next decade, it seems, Macedonian influence was on the increase, promoted by the sympathy of Knossos, Gortyn and Kydonia. The city of Lyttos was, however, favourable to Sparta; and the Spartans in 333 B.C. sent an expedition to Crete, no doubt to counter the influence of Macedon. Spartan influence is more

[3] Tarn and Griffith, HC 121; cf. p. 70.

marked in the early decades of the following century. Spartans acted as mediators in a treaty—of uncertain date, but perhaps not later than 275 B.C.—between the cities of Phalasarna and Polyrhenia, under the leadership of Kleonymos, son of Kleomenes II. When the Gortynians were involved in war in 272 B.C. they were supported by the intervention of King Areus. At roughly this time too the people of Polyrhenia dedicated a statue to Areus. Pyrrhos made an attack on Sparta in the absence of Areus and the Spartans would have been willing to send their women to Crete had the women themselves not opposed the project. The son of Pyrrhos was killed by a Cretan called Oryssos from Aptera who was fighting in the Spartan army.

In the subsequent decade the influence of another foreign power, Egypt, increased. In fact there is evidence at this time of an actual Egyptian occupation of Itanos in the east, to serve presumably as an outpost against the Macedonians. Ptolemy III (247–221 B.C.) was honoured at Eleutherna and Phalasarna; and Egyptian influence spread to other cities such as Rhithymna, Aptera, Dreros and Olous. The Chremonidean War (267/6–261 B.C.) was waged against Antigonos by Athens, Sparta and Ptolemy. There were a number of Cretan states—perhaps including Gortyn, Itanos, Olous, Aptera, Rhithymna, Polyrhenia, Phalasarna and Lyttos—which were on the side of King Areus and the Spartans in the anti-Macedonian camp, while Knossos, Kydonia and Praisos favoured the Macedonians.

Between 260 and 240 B.C. the power of Knossos seems to have been dominant, to judge from agreements made with Miletos and three different groupings of cities concerning the liberation of citizens captured by Cretan and Milesian pirates. The agreement with Knossos was binding on allied states, Tylisians, Rhaukians, Chersonesians, Milatians, Eltynians, Herakleotes, Priansians, Apolloniates, Petraians, Itanians, Praisians, Istronians, Olountians, Drerians, Latians, Eleuthernaians, Axians, Kydoniates and Phalasarnians. The allies of Gortyn included the Lyttians, Arkades, Ariaians and Hyrtaians, making up the second group. The third was headed by Phaistos in alliance with the Matalians and Polyrhenians.

Such divisions among the cities continued to exist even when, in 229/8 B.C., Athens managed to conclude a friendly agreement with them. However, in 221 B.C., Gortyn and Knossos did make a settlement which brought Crete under their sway. But this settlement was quickly brought to an end by rebellious Lyttos and the subsequent Lyttian War of 221–219 B.C.,[4] which was responsible for causing the migration of many Cretans to Miletos.

In 220 B.C., Polyrhenia and Lappa, allied to Lyttos, sought assistance from the Macedonians and Achaeans who were ranged against the Aetolians. Knossos, ally of the Aetolians, was in turn supported by the Rhodians. Troops were sent from both sides in Crete to join the forces of these external powers; and even when the Lyttian War was over, internal strife in Crete went on for some years until, in 217/16 B.C., King Philip of Macedon was able to win Crete over to his patronage for more than a decade, although Knossos and other allies of Rhodes were perhaps reluctant partners in the new arrangement. In fact there is doubt whether Crete enjoyed uninterrupted peace even during this short period. In any case, there was further war between 205/4 and 201 B.C., after Philip had embroiled the Cretans with Rhodes. But this so-called Cretan War belies its name, being conducted apparently, as we have noticed, without any central direction but as a series of raids by some states. By the end of the war, Rhodes had been able to persuade some cities to change their policies to neutrality or friendship; and it seems that the Cretans were again divided into pro-Macedonian and anti-Macedonian camps, the former including Axos, Sybrita, Lato, Istron, the Arcadians and Allaria, the latter Knossos, Polyrhenia, Kydonia and Rhaukos.

After the beginning of the second century B.C., there is growing evidence of Roman intervention in Cretan affairs. As was mentioned in the previous chapter, King Nabis of Sparta disposed of a force of 2,000 Cretans in his army which opposed Flamininus in 195 B.C. The peace terms offered to the Spartan king in that year indicate that the Romans were anxious to sabotage the cordial arrangements which existed between Sparta and certain of the Cretan states. Later on, at various times and with varying degrees of success, Roman representatives attempted to arbitrate in the repeated conflicts between Gortyn and Knossos which form the principal feature of the political

[4] See pp. 72–3.

history of Crete in those times. Thus, in 189 B.C., the praetor Q. Fabius Labeo failed in his attempt to bring hostilities to an end. He was also trying to negotiate the return of a large number of Roman captives which were held by Cretan states. Here he was a little more successful—at least he was able to reach an agreement with one state, Gortyn. In 184 B.C., however, the Cretans allowed a Roman diplomatic mission under Appius Claudius to arbitrate in their continuing quarrels. Two slices of Knossian territory had been appropriated by Gortyn and handed over to Rhaukos and Lyttos. The Gortynians were now persuaded to restore these territories; and a dispute between two other cities, Kydonia and Phalasarna, was also ended. Ten years later, when there was renewed warfare, the Romans failed to bring about a settlement. Moreover, in the course of the war between Rome and Perseus (Third Macedonian War, 171–168 B.C.) the Cretans, as we have seen, were able to conduct their quarrels on a larger scale by participating on both sides. But the war between the Cretan cities (temporarily united against any attempt to end their piratical ventures) and the Rhodians, allied with Attalus II, in 155–153 B.C., was perhaps concluded as a result of Roman diplomatic intervention.

The outbreak of the Third Macedonian War coincided with renewed conflict inside Crete, of a kind which was to be repeated time and again, with undiminished ferocity, over the next hundred years. In 171 B.C., the Kydonians attacked their ally Apollonia, to whom they were bound by solemn treaty obligations. They captured their city, killed the men and divided among themselves the women, the children, the city and its land. Then the Gortynians, in support of Apollonia, attacked Kydonia which almost succumbed (170 or 169 B.C.). The Kydonians then appealed to their ally Eumenes of Pergamon, who sent troops to occupy the city in return for their protection; and, now that Gortyn had intervened, Knossos took possession of Apollonia. This action caused further dissension between Knossos and Gortyn, but the matter was settled by treaty, concluded through the arbitration of Ptolemy Philometor, as a result of which Apollonia was transferred to Gortyn (168–166/5 B.C.). As soon as they had settled their differences, Knossos and Gortyn united to make trouble for others. They overcame Rhaukos and divided its territory between themselves (166/5

B.C.). It was probably some years afterwards that Phaistos was razed by the Gortynians.

There was another war between Knossos and Gortyn in 121/20 B.C. The Gortynians were quickly defeated, but the conflict between the two cities broke out again in 115 B.C., and lasted for several years until a settlement was reached with the help of Roman diplomacy. Since Lato and Itanos were allies of Knossos, and Olous and Hierapytna allies of Gortyn, these four cities also became involved and there was war between Lato and Olous and between Itanos and Hierapytna. Shortly before the struggle with Itanos, the Hierapytnians destroyed Praisos.[5]

This record of incessant strife justifies Strabo in his conclusion that Knossos and Gortyn had to co-operate to ensure the subjection of the rest of Crete and that strife ensued throughout Crete whenever they were at loggerheads.[6] But co-operation between the two most powerful states never lasted for long. Nor was it possible for one of them to outstrip its rival and so be in a position to enforce some kind of unity upon all the rest. Instead the cities were repeatedly divided into hostile groups and factions. When there was not open war there was only uneasy peace. There was but a single counterbalancing influence to offset this dismal general situation throughout the Hellenistic period. Elsewhere in Greece smaller states had grouped themselves into various kinds of federal unions. In Crete, too, a loose federal organization existed in Hellenistic times, the Cretan *Koinon*. This federation had a Council, composed of delegates from member states and also a popular Assembly formed by the citizens of member states. The *Koinon* was convened in different cities and its decrees were issued by Council and Assembly in conjunction. Naturally, Knossos and Gortyn were the dominant members.

However, the Cretan *Koinon* was different from other Hellenistic federations such as the Achaean League. There is no indication that it ever embraced the concept of Cretan citizenship, of a federal army or of federal magistrates. In fact, documents relevant to the *Koinon* are dated by reference to the principal magistrates of Knossos and Gortyn and there were no federal magistrates to conduct diplomatic missions. For member

---

[5] For detailed references in this complex narrative of feud and intrigue see Willetts, ASAC 234–41.        [6] 10.478.

states possessed a large measure of independence in foreign policy and confederate policies were not automatically binding upon them.[7]

Thus an apparatus did exist which could have fostered a Cretan unity if conditions had been different. But the autonomous cities were plagued by the irreconcilable contradictions of their social order. Once Cretan isolation had been broken down these contradictions became intensified. Resistant to all change, they became more and more at the mercy of forces they could not hope to control, their rivalries sharpened by the intervention of much stronger states. Occasionally, as we saw, this diplomatic influence was actually accompanied by the despatch of a garrison to the city which had sought the good offices of an external power. It was the Romans who eventually followed these examples to a logical conclusion. The Cretans were accused of sympathy with Mithridates, of supplying mercenaries and supporting piracy, in covert agreement with Cilicians and Pamphylians, and in consequence became embroiled in war with Rome. A first attempt at subjugation was so vigorously resisted, however, that the Cretans were able to make the Romans agree to peace on unfavourable terms in 71 B.C. The agreement was subsequently repudiated and the Cretans were provoked by demands of such a kind that they were obliged to refuse. This refusal furnished the excuse for the despatch of Quintus Metellus (afterwards called Creticus) to Crete to bring about the aim of Roman occupation. He was ruthlessly successful and Crete thus became in 67 B.C. the last centre of Greek independence to fall under Roman rule.

Crete as a Roman province was incorporated with Cyrene, and Gortyn became the provincial capital. The island supplied corn to Rome. A beginning was made under the early Roman Empire by St. Paul and his disciple Titus towards the wholesale Christianization of Crete; and when the partition of the Empire occurred, Crete became part of the Eastern or Byzantine Empire.

The Roman occupation can easily be invested with an air of doomed inevitability, a final act in a protracted drama of crisis and decay. But the fierce resistance of the Cretans against the invasion relieves their otherwise depressing history in the last centuries before the Christian era. Nor was that resistance vain

[7] See further Van der Mijnsbrugge, CK; cf. Willetts, ASAC 225–34.

or final, if we look upon it as the first episode in a long struggle for independence whish lasted until modern times, against other invaders and occupiers who, like the Romans, came and had their day. It seems proper then to conclude with an outline of the subsequent history of Crete, if we are to set its ancient history in the Classical and Hellenistic periods in proper focus, and not view it merely as a long twilight of decline and fall from the faded glories of a distant past.

Crete was, both strategically and commercially, of distinct importance within the Byzantine Empire. But it was lost to the Empire for more than a century when, in the reign of Michael II, about A.D. 823, it was invaded by Arab emigrants from Spain to Egypt. These Arabs came from Alexandria and they destroyed most of the cities of Crete. But they founded a new city on the site of Candia (Heraklion), which name came later to be used for the whole island. Once more Crete became a haunt of pirates who plundered the Aegean islands and coastal areas. The Byzantines and the Arabs continued to dispute the possession of Crete until it was eventually recaptured by the Byzantine general and future emperor, Nikephoros Phokas, in 961. Little trace remained of the Saracen occupation: the Mohammedan religion imposed during their stay was suppressed.

Crete was again captured in 1204, this time by Crusaders, and it was sold by their leader, Boniface, Marquis of Montferrat, to Venice. This Venetian period of Cretan history lasted until 1670. For the Venetians Crete was valuable as a centre for commanding the east Mediterranean trade routes. But, although the island had been sold, it was not so easily subdued. There was much resistance to the Venetians and many revolts. In fact, the the greater part of Crete was not finally in Venetian control until 1343. Even then the Sphakiot mountaineers continued to resist for more than twenty years. However, the Venetians were subsequently able to consolidate their possession of the island for about two centuries. Colonists from Italy began to arrive in Crete as early as 1212. Land was divided into State, Church and private property. This private section was allotted in fief to 545 noble Venetian families. The Venetians exploited the island to their advantage, largely at the expense of the downtrodden peasant serfs.

The Turks made various incursions against Crete in the

course of the sixteenth century, as part of their expansionist designs and as a means of crippling Venice, now very dependent on Cretan trade and resources. These probing expeditions were a prelude to the Turkish conquest which began in 1645 with the investment of the fortress of Ayioi Theodoroi by an army 50,000 strong. Meeting with no success there, the army landed in the bay of Khania and took the town. In 1646 they captured Rhethimnon and two years later the Venetians had lost most of Crete except for Heraklion and the fortified coastal islands. The famous siege of Heraklion began in 1648 and was continued for more than twenty years. It ended in 1669 with Crete a wholly Turkish possession, except for three fortified islands which also had eventually to be abandoned by the Venetians. Under the Turkish domination from 1670 Crete was badly governed, and endured a further period of intensified exploitation until, with the outbreak of the Greek War of Independence in 1821, a new upsurge of Cretan resistance began. There was constant unrest throughout the nineteenth century and, as Turkish power declined, Crete became a focus of the attention of the major European states. In 1898 the last Turkish soldiers left Crete, after the principal ports had been occupied by British, Russian, French and Italian forces and after the Turks had vainly attacked the British garrison in Heraklion. At the end of the year Prince George of Greece became the High Commissioner of an independent Crete.

This period of autonomy lasted from 1898 until 1913, dominated by the personality of the famous Cretan statesman Eleutherios Venizelos, leader of the Cretan Liberal party, who became Prime Minister of Greece in 1910. When war broke out between Greece and Turkey in October 1912, the movement for the union of Crete with Greece was successful. Venizelos admitted Cretan deputies to the Greek Parliament a few days before war was declared and the union was formally acknowledged by Turkey in the Treaty of London on 30 May 1913.

Like the rest of Greece, Crete underwent a period of Nazi occupation during the Second World War, heralded by the paratroop attack which began on 20 May 1941. The invasion brought much destruction and suffering in its wake, but once again the Cretans distinguished themselves by their heroic resistance. This latest episode of foreign domination came to an end with the defeat of Germany on 8 May 1945.

# Chronological Table

| Date | Crete | Greece | Ancient Egypt | |
|------|-------|--------|---------------|---|
| 5000 B.C. | Neolithic | | | |
| 3000 B.C. | Post-Neolithic | Neolithic | Early Dynastic Period | ⎧ Dynasty I<br>⎩ Dynasty II |
| 2850 B.C. | | | | |
| 2750 B.C. | | | | ⎧ Dynasty III |
| 2600 B.C. | | | Old Kingdom | Dynasty IV |
| 2500 B.C. | ⎧ Early Minoan I | ⎧ Early Helladic I | | Dynasty V |
| 2400 B.C. | ⎩ | ⎩ | | ⎩ Dynasty VI |
| 2200 B.C. | ⎧ Early Minoan II | ⎧ Early Helladic II | | |
| 2100 B.C. | | | First Intermediate Period | ⎧ Dynasties VII to X |
| 2050 B.C. | ⎧ Early Minoan III | Early Helladic III | | |
| 1950 B.C. | | | | ⎧ |

160

# CHRONOLOGICAL TABLE

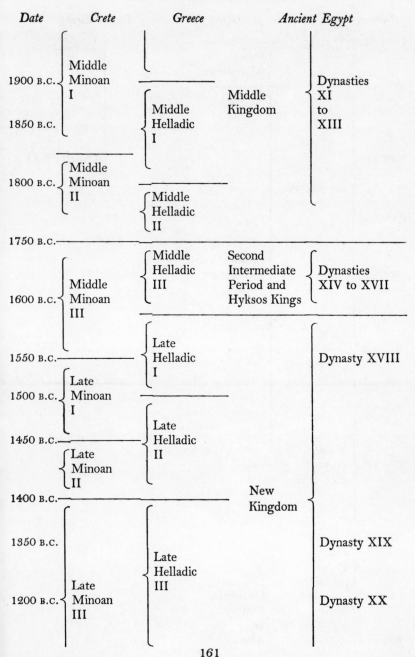

| Date | Crete | Greece | | Ancient Egypt |
|---|---|---|---|---|
| 1900 B.C. | Middle Minoan I | | Middle Kingdom | Dynasties XI to XIII |
| 1850 B.C. | | Middle Helladic I | | |
| 1800 B.C. | Middle Minoan II | | | |
| | | Middle Helladic II | | |
| 1750 B.C. | | | | |
| 1600 B.C. | Middle Minoan III | Middle Helladic III | Second Intermediate Period and Hyksos Kings | Dynasties XIV to XVII |
| 1550 B.C. | | Late Helladic I | | Dynasty XVIII |
| 1500 B.C. | Late Minoan I | | | |
| 1450 B.C. | | Late Helladic II | | |
| | Late Minoan II | | | |
| 1400 B.C. | | | New Kingdom | |
| 1350 B.C. | | Late Helladic III | | Dynasty XIX |
| 1200 B.C. | Late Minoan III | | | Dynasty XX |

161

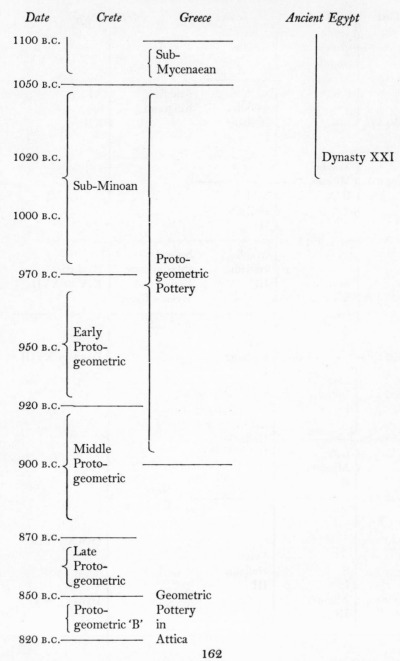

| Date | Crete | Greece | Ancient Egypt |
|---|---|---|---|
| 1100 B.C. | | Sub-Mycenaean | |
| 1050 B.C. | | | |
| 1020 B.C. | Sub-Minoan | | Dynasty XXI |
| 1000 B.C. | | | |
| 970 B.C. | | Proto-geometric Pottery | |
| 950 B.C. | Early Proto-geometric | | |
| 920 B.C. | | | |
| 900 B.C. | Middle Proto-geometric | | |
| 870 B.C. | | | |
| 850 B.C. | Late Proto-geometric | Geometric Pottery in Attica | |
| 820 B.C. | Proto-geometric 'B' | | |

| Date | Crete | Greece |
|------|-------|--------|
| 800 B.C. | Early Geometric | |
| 776 B.C. | Mature Geometric | First Olympiad |
| 770 B.C. | | |
| 750 B.C. | Late Geometric | |
| 735 B.C. | Early Orientalizing | |
| 700 B.C. | Late Orientalizing | |
| 650 B.C. | Archaic Period | |
| 530 B.C. | Classical Period | |
| 330 B.C. | | |
| 67 B.C. | Hellenistic Period Roman Conquest | |
| 323 A.D. | Graeco-Roman Period | |
| 828 A.D.(?) | Crete captured by Saracens. | |
| 961 A.D. | Crete recaptured by Nikephoros Phokas | |
| 1204 A.D. | Crete captured by Crusaders | |
| 1210 A.D. | Venetian governor appointed | |

163

# Bibliography

Where an English translation of a foreign work is specified, the references are to its pages. Lists of epigraphical publications and of periodicals, with the abbreviations used for them, are given at the end of the bibliography.

ALEXIOU, S. Ἡ μινωϊκὴ θεὰ μεθ' ὑψωμένων χειρῶν, ΚΚ (1958).

ALLBAUGH, L. G. *Crete: A Case Study of an Underdeveloped Area*. Princeton, 1953.

ALLEN, T. W., HALLIDAY, W. R., and SIKES, E. E. *Homeric Hymns*. 2nd ed. Oxford, 1936.

ALY, W. *Der kretische Apollonkult*. Leipzig, 1908.

AUTRAN, C. *La préhistoire du Christianisme*. Paris, 1941.

BACHOFEN, J. J. *Das Mütterrecht*. Stuttgart, 1861.

BANTI, L. *Myth in Pre-Classical Art*. AJA 58.

BARNETT, R. D. *The Epic of Kumarbi and the Theogony of Hesiod*. JHS 65.

BAUDISSIN, W. W. *Kyrios als Gottesname im Judentum und seine Stelle in der Religionsgeschichte*. Giessen, 1929.

BAUNACK, J. and T. *Die Inschrift von Gortyn*. Leipzig, 1885.

BAUR, P. V. C. *Eileithyia: The University of Missouri Studies* I:4. 1902.

BAYNES, N. H. *The Byzantine Empire*. London, 1926.

BEATTIE, A. J. *A Plain Guide to the Ventris Decipherment of the Mycenaean Linear B Script. Mitteilungen des Instituts für Orientforschung*. 6.I (1958).

—— *Mr. Ventris' Decipherment of the Minoan Linear B Script*. JHS 76.

—— *The 'Spice' Tablets of Cnossos, Pylos and Mycenae* in *Minoica*. 6–34.

BECHTEL, F. *Die griechischen Dialekte*. Berlin, 1921–4.

BELOCH, K. J. *Griechische Geschichte*. 2nd ed. Strasbourg, 1912–27.

BELON, P. *Obseruations sur plusieurs singularitez*. Paris, 1553.

BÉRARD, J. *Les Hyksos et la légende d'Io*. S 29.

BERNHÖFT, F. *Die Inschrift von Gortyn*. Stuttgart, 1886.

BISCHOFF, H. RE s.v. *Kalender*.

BITTEL, K. *Die Ruinen von Bogazköy der Haupstadt des Hethiterreichs*. Berlin/Leipzig, 1937.

BLASS, F. *Die kretischen Inschriften*, in SGDI III.2.3, 227–423. Göttingen, 1905.

BLEGEN, C. W. *The Coming of the Greeks.* AJA 32.

BLINKENBERG, C. *The Thunder-weapon in Religion and Folklore.* Cambridge, 1911.

BOARDMAN, J. *The Cretan Collection in Oxford.* Oxford, 1961.

BOISACQ, E. *Dictionnaire étymologique de la langue grecque.* 4th ed. Heidelberg, 1950.

BONNER, R. J., and SMITH, G. *The Administration of Justice from Homer to Aristotle.* Chicago, 1930–8.

BOSANQUET, R. C. *The Palaikastro Hymn of the Kouretes.* ABSA 15.

BOSSERT, H. T. *Die Beschwörung einer Krankheit in der Sprache von Kreta.* OL 34.

—— *The Art of Ancient Crete.* London, 1937.

BOWRA, C. M. *Greek Lyric Poetry.* 2nd ed. Oxford, 1961.

—— *Heroic Poetry.* London, 1952.

—— *Homer and his Forerunners.* Edinburgh, 1955.

BRANDENSTEIN, W. *Bermerkungen zur Völkertafel in der Genesis, Festschrift Debrunner.* Bern, 1954, 66–70.

BRAUSE, J. *Lautlehre der kretischen Dialekte.* Halle, 1909.

BRÉAL, M. *Un ancien texte de loi de la Crète,* RA 36.

BRIFFAULT, R. *The Mothers.* London, 1927.

BROCK, J. K. *Fortetsa.* Cambridge, 1957.

BROOKS, E. W. *The Arab Occupation of Crete. English Historical Review* 28 (1913), pp. 431–43.

BÜCHELER, F., and ZITELMANN, E. *Das Recht von Gortyn,* RM 40.

BÜCHER, K. *Arbeit und Rhythmus.* 5th ed. Leipzig, 1919.

BUCK, C. D. *Comparative Grammar of Greek and Latin.* Chicago, 1933.

—— *The Greek Dialects.* Chicago, 1955.

BUDGE, E. A. W. *The Gods of the Egyptians.* London, 1904.

BURKITT, M. C. *Prehistory.* 2nd ed. Cambridge, 1925.

BURN, A. R. *The Lyric Age of Greece.* London, 1960.

BURY, J. B. *History of Greece.* 3rd ed. by R. Meiggs, London, 1951.

BUSOLT, G. *Griechische Staatskunde,* in I. von Müller's *Handbuch der klassischen Altertums-Wissenschaft,* IV. 1.1. 3rd ed. Munich, 1920–6.

CALHOUN, G. M. *Growth of Criminal Law in Ancient Greece.* Berkeley, 1927.

*Cambridge Ancient History.* Cambridge, 1925–39.

CARDINALI, G. *Crete e le grandi potenze ellenistiche sino alla guerra di Litto, Rivista di storia antica 9.*

—— *Creta nel tramonto dell'Ellenismo,* RF 35.

—— *La guerra di Litto,* RF 33.

CARNOY, A. *Dictionnaire étymologique du proto-indo-européen.* Louvain, 1955.

CARY, M. *Geographic Background of Greek and Roman History.* Oxford, 1949.

CHADWICK, H. M. *The Growth of Literature.* Cambridge, 1925–39.

―― *The Heroic Age.* Cambridge, 1912.

CHADWICK, J. *The Greek Dialects and Greek Pre-History*, GR 3.1.

―― *The Prehistory of the Greek Language. Cambridge Ancient History* (rev. ed.), 2.39, 1963.

CHAMOUX, F. *Cyrène sous la monarchie des Battiades.* Paris, 1953.

CHANTRAINE, P. *Grammaire homérique.* Paris, 1942.

―― *Études sur le vocabulaire grec.* Paris, 1956.

―― *Morphologie historique du grec.* Paris, 1945.

CHAPOUTHIER, F. (and others), *Fouilles exécutées à Mallia* (Rapports 1, 2, 3). Paris, 1928–42.

CHARBONNEAUX, J. *Tholos et prytanée*, BCH 49.

CHILDE, V. G. *The Aryans.* London, 1926.

―― *The Bronze Age.* Cambridge, 1930.

―― *The Bronze Age*, PP 12.

―― *The Date and Origin of Minyan Ware.* JHS 35.

―― *The Dawn of European Civilization.* 6th ed. London, 1957.

―― *History.* London, 1947.

―― *Piecing Together the Past.* London, 1956.

―― *The Prehistory of European Society.* London, 1958.

―― *Progress and Archaeology.* London, 1944.

―― *What Happened in History.* 2nd ed. Harmondsworth, 1954.

CHISHULL, E. *Antiquitates Asiaticae.* London, 1728.

CHRIMES, K. M. T. *Ancient Sparta.* Manchester, 1949.

CLARK, G. *From Savagery to Civilization.* London, 1946.

CLARK, R. T. RUNDLE. *Myth and Symbol in Ancient Egypt.* London, 1959.

COHEN, R. *La Grèce et l'hellénisation du monde antique.* 2nd ed. Paris, 1939.

COLLIGNON, L. M. *Les colleges de 'Neoi' dans les cités grecques, Annales de la faculté des lettres de Bordeaux.* 2, 1880.

COLLINGWOOD, R. G. *The Idea of History.* Oxford, 1946.

COMPARETTI, D. *Le Leggi di Gortyna e le altre iscrizioni arcaiche cretesi edite ed illustrate.* MA 3.

COOK, A. B. *Zeus.* Cambridge, 1914–40.

―― *Who Was the Wife of Zeus?* CR 20.

―― *Zeus, Jupiter and the Oak.* CR 17.

COOK, S. A. *The Religion of Ancient Palestine in the Light of Archaeology.* London, 1930.

CORNFORD, F. M. *The Ἀπαρχαί and the Eleusinian Mysteries* in Quiggin 153.

―― *The Origin of the Olympic Games* in Harrison, T. 212.

―― *Principium Sapientiae.* Cambridge, 1952.

CORTSEN, S. P. *Die Lemnische Inschrift, Gl.* 18.

CROISET, A. and M. *Histoire de la littérature grecque.* 3rd ed. Paris, 1901–21.

DAREMBERG, C., and SAGLIO, E. *Dictionnaire des antiquités grecques et romaines.* Paris, 1877–1919.

DARESTE, R. *Le χρεωφυλάκιον dans les villes grecques,* BCH 6.

DAWKINS, R. M. *The Sanctuary of Artemis Orthia at Sparta.* London, 1929.

DE SANCTIS, G. *Storia dei Greci dalle origini alla fine del secolo V.* Florence, 1939.

——*The* Startus *in the Cretan Inscriptions.* AJA 5 (1901).

DEITERS, P. *De Cretensium titulis publicis quaestiones epigraphicae.* Diss. Jena, 1904.

DEMARGNE. P. *La Crète dédalique.* Paris, 1947.

—— and VAN EFFENTERRE, H. *Recherches à Dréros,* BCH, 61.

DEMETRAKOS, D. Μέγα λεξικὸν τῆς ἑλληνικῆς γλιώσσης Athens, 1936.

DESBOROUGH, V. R. D'A. *Protogeometric Pottery.* Oxford, 1952.

——*The Last Mycenaeans and Their Successors.* Oxford, 1964.

DEUBNER, L. *Attische Feste.* Berlin, 1932.

DIAMOND, A. S. *Primitive Law.* 2nd ed. London, 1950.

—— *The Evolution of Law and Order.* London, 1951.

DIETERICH, A. *Mutter Erde.* Leipzig/Berlin, 1905.

DIKAIOS, P. *The Excavations at Vounous-Bellapais in Cyprus, 1931–2.* *Arc.* 88.

DILLER, A. *A New Source on the Spartan* Ephebia, AJP 62.

DODDS, E. R. *The Greeks and the Irrational.* Oxford, 1951.

DOUBLET, G. *Inscriptions de Crète.* BCH 13.

DUNBABIN, T. J. *The Greeks and their Eastern Neighbours.* London, 1957.

DURKHEIM, E. *Les formes élémentaires de la vie religieuse.* 2nd ed. Paris, 1912.

EARTHY, E. D. *Valenge Women.* Oxford, 1933.

EDELSTEIN, E. J. and L. *Asclepius: A Collection and Interpretation of the Testimonies.* Baltimore, 1945.

EGGER, A. E. *Études historiques sur les traités publics.* 2nd ed. Paris, 1866.

EHRENBERG, V. *The Greek State.* Oxford, 1960.

—— *The People of Aristophanes.* 2nd ed. Oxford, 1951.

ELDERKIN, G. W. *The Marriage of Zeus and Hera.* AJA 41.

ELDERKIN, K. M. *Jointed Dolls in Antiquity.* AJA 34.

ENGELS, F. *Der Ursprung der Familie, des Privateigentums und des Staats.* (Marx-Engels Gesamtausgabe.) *Origin of the Family, Private Property and the State.* London, 1940.

ENGNELL, I. *Studies in Divine Kingship in the Ancient Near East.* Uppsala, 1943.

EVANS, A. J. *Knossos Excavations, 1903.* ABSA 9.

EVANS, A. J. *The Mycenaean Tree and Pillar Cult.* JHS 21.
—— *The Palace of Minos.* London, 1921–35.
—— *Shaft Graves and Beehive Tombs of Mycenae.* London, 1929.
—— *The Ring of Nestor.* JHS 45.
FARNELL, G. S. *Greek Lyric Poetry.* London, 1891.
FARNELL, L. R. *Cults of the Greek States.* Oxford, 1896–1909.
—— *Greek Hero Cults.* Oxford, 1921.
FARRINGTON, B. *Head and Hand in Ancient Greece.* London, 1947.
FAURE, P. *Fonctions des cavernes crétoises.* Paris, 1964.
FERGUSON, W. S. *The Zulus and the Spartans: A Comparison of their Military Systems,* HAS 2.
FICK, A. *Hattiden und Danubier in Griechenland.* Göttingen, 1909.
—— *Vorgriechische Ortsnamen als Quelle für die Vorgeschichte Griechenlands.* Göttingen, 1905.
FINLEY, M. I. *Between Slavery and Freedom* in *Comparative Studies in Society and History* Vol. VI. No. 3 (April 1964), pp. 233–49.
—— *Studies in Land and Credit in Ancient Athens, 500–200 B.C.* New Brunswick, 1951.
—— *The Servile Statuses of Ancient Greece* in *Revue Internationale des Droits de l'Antiquité. 3e Serie, Tome VII.* 1960
—— *The World of Odysseus.* London, 1956.
FONTENROSE, J. *Python.* Berkeley/Los Angeles, 1959.
FORBES, C. A. *Neoi: A Contribution to the Study of Greek Associations* (Philological Monographs published by the American Philological Association, No. 2). Middletown, Connecticut, 1933.
FORMAN, W. and B., and POULÍK, J. *Prehistoric Art.* London, 1955.
FORREST, G. *The First Sacred War.* BCH 80.
FORSDYKE, J. *Greece before Homer.* London, 1956.
—— *Minos of Crete.* JWCI 15.
—— *The Pottery called Minyan Ware.* JHS 34.
FOTHERINGHAM, J. K. *Cleostratus.* JHS 39.
FRANKFORT, H. *Cylinder Seals.* London, 1939.
—— *Kingship and the Gods.* Chicago, 1948.
FRAZER, J. G. *Apollodorus.* London, 1921.
—— *Folklore and the Old Testament.* London, 1919.
—— *Lectures on the Early History of the Kingship.* London, 1905.
—— *Pausanias's Description of Greece.* London, 1898.
—— *The Golden Bough.* London, 1923–7.
—— *The Prytaneum, The Temple of Vesta, The Vestals, Perpetual Fires,* JP 14.
—— *Totemica.* London, 1937.
—— *Totemism and Exogamy.* London, 1910.
FREEMAN, K. J. *Schools of Hellas.* 3rd ed. by M. J. Rendall, London, 1922.

FRÖDIN, O., and PERSSON, A. W. *Asine*. Stockholm, 1938.

FROST, K. T. *The Critias and Minoan Crete*. JHS 33.

FURTWÄNGLER, A. *Aegina. Das Heiligtum der Aphaia*. Munich, 1906.

GARDNER, P. *The Types of Greek Coins*. Cambridge, 1883.

GEMOLL, A. *Das Recht von Gortyn*. Striegau, 1889.

GEORGIEV, V. *Les deux langues des inscriptions Crétoises en Linéaire A*. Sophia, 1963.

GLOTZ, G. *La civilisation égéenne*. Paris, 1923. *Aegean Civilization*. London, 1926.

—— *La cité grecque*. Paris, 1928.

—— *La solidarité de la famille dans le droit criminel en Grèce*. Paris, 1904.

—— *Le travail dans la Grèce ancienne*. Paris, 1920. *Ancient Greece at Work*. London, 1926.

GOMME, A. W. *Population of Athens in the Fifth and Fourth Centuries B.C.* Oxford, 1933.

GORDON, C. H. *Ugaritic Handbook*. Rome, 1947.

—— *Ugaritic Literature*. Rome, 1949.

—— *Ugaritic Manual*. Rome, 1955.

GRIFFITH, G. T. *The Mercenaries of the Hellenistic World*. Cambridge, 1935.

GROENEWEGEN-FRANKFORT, A. H. *Arrest and Movement*. Chicago, 1951.

GRÖNBECH, V. *Culture of the Teutons*. Oxford, 1931.

GROTE, G. *History of Greeece*. London, 1846.

GRUMACH, E. *Bemerkungen zu M. Ventris—J. Chadwick, Evidence for Greek Dialect in the Mycenaean Archives*. OL 52.7/8.

———— (ed.) *Minoica*. Berlin, 1958.

GRUPPE, O. *Griechische Mythologie und Religionsgeschichte*. Munich, 1906.

GUARDUCCI, M. *Demiurgi in Creta*, RF 8 (1930).

—— *Eunomia, Historia* 7.

—— *Intorno ai perieci di Creta*, RF 14 (1936).

—— *Note sul calendario cretese, Ephigraphica* 7.72.

—— *Note sul KOINON cretese*, RF 28 (1950).

—— *Una nuova confederazione cretese: gli Orioi*, RF 16 (1938).

GUIRAUD, P. *La propriété foncière en Grèce jusqu'a la conquête romaine*. Paris, 1893.

GURNEY, O. R. *The Hittites*. London, 1952.

GUTHRIE, W. K. C. *Early Greek Religion in the Light of the Decipherment of Linear B*. BICS 6.

—— *Orpheus and Greek Religion*. 2nd ed. London, 1952.

—— *The Greeks and their Gods*. London, 1950.

HALBHERR, F. *Cretan Expedition*. AJA 9 (1894), 11 (1896), 1 (1897), 2 (1898), 5 (1901).

HALBHERR, F. *Iscrizioni cretesi, Mus. It. 3.*

—— and COMPARETTI, D. *Epigrafi archaiche di varie città cretesi, Mus. It. 2.*

—— and FABRICIUS, E. *Leggi antiche della città di Gortyna.* Florence, 1885.

HALEY, J. B. *The Coming of the Greeks.* AJA 32.

HALL, H. R. *The Civilization of Greece in the Bronze Age.* London, 1928.

HALLIDAY, W. R. *The Hybristika.* ABSA 16.

HAMMOND, N. G. L. *A History of Greece.* Oxford, 1959.

HANSEN, H. D. *Early Civilization in Thessaly.* Baltimore, 1933.

HARRISON, J. E. *Myths of the Odyssey.* London, 1882.

—— *Prolegomena to the Study of Greek Religion.* 3rd ed. Cambridge, 1922.

—— *Primitive Hero Worship*, CR 6.474, 7.74.

—— *Sophocles' Ichneutae and the Dromena of Kyllene and the Satyrs.* Quiggin 136.

—— *The Kouretes and Zeus Kouros.* ABSA 15.

—— *Themis.* 2nd ed. Cambridge, 1927.

HARTLAND, E. S. *Primitive Paternity.* London, 1909–10.

HASEBROEK, J. *Staat und Handel in alten Griechenland.* Tübingen, 1928. *Trade and Politics in Ancient Greece.* London, 1933.

HASLUCK, F. W. *Cyzicus.* Cambridge, 1910.

HASTINGS, J. *Encyclopaedia of Ethics and Religion.* Edinburgh, 1908–18.

HAUSSOULLIER, B. *Inscriptions d'Aptéra (Crète)*, BCH 3.

—— *Inscriptions de Crète*, BCH 3.

HAWES, MRS. H. A. (BOYD). *Excavations at Gournia, Crete* (By Harriet A. Boyd). Washington, 1908.

HAWKES, C. F. C. *The Prehistoric Foundations of Europe.* London, 1940.

HAZZIDAKIS, J. *Tylissos à l'époque minoenne.* Paris, 1921.

HEAD, B. V. *Historia Numorum.* 2nd ed. Oxford, 1911.

HEADLAM, J. W. *The Procedure of the Gortynian Inscription.* JHS 13.

HEICHELHEIM, F. *Wirtschaftsgeschichte des Altertums.* Leiden, 1939. *An Ancient Economic History I.* Leiden, 1958.

HERZOG, R. Κρητικὸς πόλεμος Κ 2.

HEURTLEY, W. A. *Prehistoric Macedonia.* Cambridge, 1939.

HIGNETT, C. *A History of the Athenian Constitution to the End of the Fifth Century B.C..* Oxford, 1952.

HOBHOUSE, L. T. *The Simplest Peoples.* BJS 7.2

—— WHEELER, G. C. and GINSBERG, T. *Material Culture and Social Institutions of the Simpler Peoples.* London, 1930.

HOCART, A. M. *Kingship.* Oxford, 1927.

HOECK, K. *Kreta.* Göttingen, 1823–8.

HOLLEAUX, M. *Études d'histoire hellénistique. Remarques sur les décrets des villes de Crète relatifs à l'* ἀσυλία *de Téos*, K 13.

—— *Études d'histoire hellénistique. Sur la'guerre crétoise'* (Κρητικὸς πόλεμος), REG 30.

HOLLIS, A. C. *The Masai, their Language and Folklore*. Oxford, 1905.

—— *The Nandi, their Language and Folklore*. Oxford, 1909.

HOMOLLE, T. *Comptes des hiéropes du temple d'Apollon délièn*. BCH 6.

—— *Convention entre trois villes crétoises*, BCH 3.

HOOKE, S. H. (editor). *The Labyrinth*. London, 1935.

—— *Myth and Ritual*. Oxford, 1933.

—— *Myth, Ritual and Kingship*. Oxford, 1958.

HOW, W. W., and WELLS, J. A. *A Commentary on Herodotus*. 2nd ed. Oxford, 1928.

HUTCHINSON, R. W. *Prehistoric Crete*. Harmondsworth, 1962.

JARDÉ, A. *Les céréales dans l'antiquité grecque I*. Paris, 1925.

JEANMAIRE, H. *Couroi et Courètes*. Lille, 1939.

—— *Dionysos*. Paris, 1951.

—— *La cryptie lacédémonienne*. REG. 26.

JEFFERY, L. H. *The Local Scripts of Archaic Greece*. Oxford, 1961.

JONES, A. H. M. *Athenian Democracy*. Oxford, 1960.

KAHRSTEDT, U. *Griechisches Staatsrecht I*. Göttingen, 1922.

KANTOR, H. J. *The Aegean and the Orient in the Second Millennium B.C.* Bloomington, 1947.

KARSTEN, R. *The Civilization of the South American Indians*. London, 1926.

KAZAMANOVA, L. N. *Ocherki sotsial'no-ekonomicheskoi istorii Krita V–IV vv. do n.e.* Moscow, 1964.

—— *Rabovladenie na Krite v VI–IV vv. do n.e.* VDI 3 (40).

KENNA, V. E. G. *Cretan Seals*. Oxford, 1960.

KIRCHHOFF, A. *Studien zur Geschichte des grieschischen Alphabets*. 4th ed. Gütersloh, 1887.

KIRK, G. S. *The Songs of Homer*. Cambridge, 1962.

KIRSTEN, E. *Die Insel Kreta im fünften und vierten Jahrundert*. Diss. Leipzig, 1936.

KLINGENDER, F. D. *Palaeolithic Religion and the Principle of Social Evolution*. BJS 5.2.

KOHLER, J., and ZIEBARTH, E. *Das Stadtrecht von Gortyn*. Göttingen, 1912.

KOVALEVSKY, M. M. *Tableau des origines de l'évolution de la famille et de la propriété*. Stockholm, 1890.

KRETSCHMER, P. *Einleitung zur Geschichte der griechischen Sprache*. Göttingen, 1896.

—— *Die Stellung der lykischen Sprache*, Gl. 27.256, 28.101.

—— *Mythische Namen*, Gl. 8.

KUBITSCHEK, W. *Grundriss der Antiken Zeitrechnung: Handb. der Altertumswissenschaft.* I, t. VII. München, 1927.

―― *Die Kalenderbücher von Florenz, Rom und Leyden, Wiener Denkschr.* Bd.57. Abh.2.

KUNZE, E. *Kretische Bronzereliefs.* Stuttgart, 1931.

LANDTMAN, G. *Origin of the Inequality of the Social Classes.* London, 1938.

LANGDON, S. *The Babylonian Epic of Creation.* Oxford, 1923.

―― *Babylonian Menologies and Semitic Calendars.* London, 1935.

LARSEN, J. A. O. *Perioeci in Crete.* CP 31.

―― *Representative Government in Greek and Roman History.* Berkeley, 1955.

―― *The Assembly of the Aetolian League,* in *Transactions of the American Philological Association* 83.

―― *The Early Achaean League,* in *Studies Presented to D. M. Robinson.*

―― *The Judgment of Antiquity on Democracy,* CP 49.

LAUNEY, M. *Le verger d'Héraklès à Thasos,* BCH 61.

LAYARD, J. *Stone Men of Malekula.* London, 1942.

LEAF, W. *Homer and History.* London, 1915.

LE BAS, P., WADDINGTON, W. H., and FOUCART, P. *Voyage archéologique en Grèce et en Asie Mineure.* Paris, 1847–70.

LEGRAND, E. *Descriptions des îles de l'Archipel par Christophe Buondelmonti.* Paris, 1897.

LEJEUNE, M. *Traité de phonétique grecque.* Paris, 1947.

LEKATSAS, P. ʽΗ Ψυχή. Athens, 1957.

LETHABY, W. R. *The Earlier Temple of Artemis at Ephesus.* JHS 37.

LEVI, D. *Gli scavi del 1954 sull' acropoli di Gortina, Annuario.* 1955–6.

―― *Gleanings from Crete.* AJA 49.

LEWY, H. *Altes Stadtrecht von Gortyn.* Berlin, 1885.

LILLEY, S. *Men, Machines and History.* London, 1948.

LLOYD, S. *Early Anatolia.* London, 1956.

LORIMER, H. L. *Homer and the Monuments.* London, 1950.

LOTZE, D. ΜΕΤΑΞΥ ΕΛΕΥΘΕΡΩΝ ΚΑΙ ΔΟΥΛΩΝ Berlin, 1959.

LOWIE, R. H. *Primitive Society.* New York, 1929.

MCDONALD, W. A. *The Political Meeting Places of the Greeks.* Baltimore, 1943.

MAINE, H. J. S. *Dissertations on Early Law and Custom.* London, 1883.

MAIURI, A. *'Eunomia' a Creta,* RL 19.

―― *Il calendario cretese.* RL 19.

―― *Studi sull' onomastica cretese.* RL 19–20.

MARINATOS, S. *The Cult of the Cretan Caves.* RR 5.

MARTHA, J. *Inscription métrique de Paros,* BCH 6.

MARX, K. *Das Kapital.* (Marx-Engels Gesamtausgabe). *Capital.* 1. London, 1938. II–III, Chicago, 1933.

—— *Pre-capitalist Economic Formations* (with an Introduction by Eric Hobsbawm). London, 1964.

MASON, O. T. *Woman's Share in Primitive Culture.* London, 1895.

MATZ, F. (ed.) *Forschungen auf Kreta 1942.* Berlin, 1951.

—— *Frühkretische Siegel.* Berlin, 1928.

—— *Kreta, Mykene, Troja.* Stuttgart, 1956.

MEILLET, A. *Aperçu d'une histoire de la langue grecque.* 4th ed. Paris, 1935.

—— *Introduction à l'étude comparative des langues indo-européennes.* 8th ed. Paris, 1937.

—— and VENDRYES, J. *Grammaire comparée des langues classiques.* 2nd ed. Paris, 1927.

MEISTER, K. *Der syntaktische Gebrauch des Genetivs in den Kretischen Dialektinschriften. Indogerman. Forsch.* 18.

MENDELSOHN, I. *Slavery in the Ancient Near East.* New York, 1949.

MERRIAM, A. C. *Law Code of the Kretan Gortyna.* AJA 1 (1885) and 2 (1886).

MEYER, E. *Geschichte des Altertums.* 2nd ed. Stuttgart, 1937.

MICHELL, H. *Economics of Ancient Greece.* 2nd ed. Cambridge, 1957.

—— *Sparta.* Cambridge, 1952.

MIROSCHNIKOFF, S. V. *Gortynskie Zakoni, Zapiski imperat. russk. archeol. obschtschesva 3.* St. Petersburg, 1888.

MOMMSEN, A. *Feste der Stadt Athen.* Leipzig, 1898.

MONTESQUIEU, C. L. *De l'esprit de lois.* (Les éditions Nagel) Paris, 1950.

MORGAN, L. H. *Ancient Society.* 2nd ed. Chicago, 1910.

MORROW, G. R. *Plato's Cretan City.* Princeton, 1960.

MÜLLER, K. *Frühmykenische Reliefs* in *Jahrb.* 30 (1915).

MÜLLER, K. O. *Die Dorier.* 2nd ed. Breslau, 1844. *The History and Antiquities of the Doric Race.* Oxford, 1830.

—— *Orchomenos und die Minyer.* 2nd ed. Breslau, 1844.

—— *Prolegomena zu einer wissenschaftlichen Mythologie.* Göttingen, 1825.

MURRAY, G. *The Hymn of the Kouretes.* ABSA 15.

—— *The Rise of the Greek Epic.* 3rd ed. Oxford, 1924.

MUTTELSEE, M. *Zur Verfassungsgeschichte Kretas im Zeitalter des Hellenismus.* Diss. Hamburg, 1925.

MYLONAS, G. E. *Ancient Mycenae.* London, 1957.

—— *Priam's Troy and the Date of its Fall. Hesperia* 33.4 (1964).

—— and RAYMOND, D. *Studies presented to D. M. Robinson.* St. Louis, 1951–3.

MYRES, J. L. *Homer and his Critics.* London, 1958.

—— *Inscriptions from Crete.* JHS 16.

—— *Who were the Greeks?* Berkeley, 1930.

NEUGEBAUER, O. *The Exact Sciences in Antiquity.* Princeton, 1952.

NILSSON, M. P. *Das frühe Griechenland von innen gesehen. Hist.* 3.3.

—— *Die Entstehung und Religiöse Bedeutung des griechischen Kalenders.* Lunds Universitets Årsskrift. N.F. Aud. 1, 14.21. Lund, 1918.

—— *Die Grundlagen des spartanischen Lebens.* K 12.

—— *Geschichte der griechischen Religion.* Munich, 1941–50.

—— *Greek Piety.* Oxford, 1948.

—— *Greek Popular Religion.* New York, 1940.

—— *Griechische Feste von religiöser Bedeutung mit Ausschluss der attischen.* Darmstadt, 1957.

—— *History of Greek Religion.* 2nd ed. Oxford, 1949.

—— *Homer and Mycenae.* London, 1933.

—— *Minoan-Mycenaean Religion.* 2nd ed. Lund, 1950.

—— *Mycenaean Origin of Greek Mythology.* London, 1932.

—— *Opuscula Selecta* 1–2. Lund. 1951–2.

—— *Primitive Time Reckoning.* Lund/Oxford, 1920.

—— *Sonnenkalendar und Sonnenreligion, Arch. f. Religionswiss.* 30.

—— *Studia de Dionysiis Atticis.* Lund, 1900.

—— *The New Inscriptions of the Salaminioi.* AJP 59.

ORMEROD, H. A. *Piracy in the Ancient World.* Liverpool–London, 1924.

OSTROGORSKY, G. *History of the Byzantine State.* Oxford, 1956.

OVERBECK, J. *Die antiken Schriftquellen z. Geschichte d. bildunden Künste bei d. Griechen.* Leipzig, 1868.

PAGE, D. L. *History and the Homeric Iliad.* Berkeley–Los Angeles, 1959.

PAPADOPOULOS, I. B. Ἡ Κρήτη ὑπὸ τοὺς Σαρακηνούς. Athens, 1948.

PALMER, L. R. *Achaeans and Indo-Europeans.* Oxford, 1955.

—— *Mycenaeans and Minoans: Aegean Prehistory in the Light of the Linear B tablets.* London, 1961.

—— *The Interpretation of Mycenaean Greek Texts.* Oxford, 1963.

—— and BOARDMAN, J. *On the Knossos Tablets.* Oxford, 1963.

PARKE, H. W. *Greek Mercenary Soldiers.* Oxford, 1933.

—— and WORMELL, D. E. W. *The Delphic Oracle.* Oxford, 1956.

PARKER, R. A. *The Calendars of Ancient Egypt.* Chicago, 1953.

PARRY, M. *Les formules et la métrique d'Homère.* Paris, 1928.

PASHLEY, R. *Travels in Crete.* Cambridge–London, 1837.

PAULY, A., WISSOWA, G., and KROLL, W. *Realencyclopädie der classischen Altertumswissenschaft.* Sutttgart, 1894–.

PENDLEBURY, J. D. S. *Archaeology of Crete.* London, 1939.

PERNIER, L., and BANTI, L. *Il palazzo minoico di Festos.* Rome, 1935–51.

PERSSON, A. W. *Der Ursprung der eleusinischen Mysterien. Arch. f. Religionswiss.* 21.

—— *The Religion of Greece in Prehistoric Times.* Berkeley/Los Angeles, 1942.

PFUHL, E. *Malerei und Zeichnung der Griechen*. Munich, 1923.

PHILLIPSON, C. *The International Law and Custom of Ancient Greece and Rome*. London, 1911.

PICARD, C. *Ephèse et Claros*. Paris, 1922.

—— *Les Origines du Polythéisme Hellénique*. Paris, 1930.

—— *Les Religions Préhelléniques*. Paris, 1948.

—— *Sur la patrie et les pérégrinations de Déméter*. REG 40.

PICKARD-CAMBRIDGE, A. *Dithyramb, Tragedy and Comedy*. Oxford, 1927.

—— *The Dramatic Festivals of Athens*. Oxford, 1953.

PLATON, N. *A Guide to the Archaeological Museum of Heraklion*. 3rd ed. Heraklion, 1959.

PÖHLMANN, R. VON. *Geschichte der sozialen Frage und des Sozialismus in der Antiken Welt*. 3rd ed. Munich, 1926.

POLAND, F. *Geschichte des griechischen Vereinswesens*. Leipzig, 1909.

POLITES, N. G. Παραδώσεις τοῦ ἑλληνικοῦ λαοῦ. Athens, 1904.

—— Παροιμίαι. Athens, 1899–1902.

PRELLER, L. VON. *Griechische Mythologie*. 4th ed. by C. Robert. Berlin, 1887–1926.

PRITCHARD, J. B. (ed.) *Ancient Near Eastern Texts*. Princeton, 1950.

*Proceedings of the Second International Congress of Classical Studies*. Copenhagen, 1958.

QUIGGIN, E. C. *Essays and Studies Presented to William Ridgeway*. Cambridge, 1913.

RAEDER, A. *L'arbitrage international chez les hellènes*. Kristiania, 1912.

RANSOME, H. M. *The Sacred Bee*. London, 1937.

RAVEN, E. J. P. *The Hierapytna Hoard of Greek and Roman Coins*, Num. Chron. 5 S. 18.

REICHEL, A. *Die Stierspiele in der kretisch-mykenischen Cultur*. AM 34.

REINACH, A. J. *Inscriptions d'Itanos*, REG 24.

RIDGEWAY, W. *The Early Age of Greece*. Cambridge, 1901–31.

—— *The Supplices of Aeschylus*, in *Cambridge Praelections*, 1906.

RIVERS, W. H. R. *Kinship and Social Organisation*. London, 1932.

ROBERT, C. *Sosipolis in Olympia*. AM 18.

ROBERT, L. *Les Asklepieis de l'Archipel*. REG 46.

ROBERTSON SMITH, W. *Religion of the Semites*. 3rd ed. London, 1927.

ROBY, H. J. *The Twelve Tables of Gortyn*. LQR 2.

RODENWALDT, G. *Tiryns*. Athens, 1912.

ROHDE, E. *Psyche: Seelencult und Unsterblichkeitsglaube der Griechen*. Freiburg, 1898.

ROSCHER, W. H. *Ausführliches Lexicon der griechischen und römischen Mythologie*. Leipzig, 1884–1937.

—— *Selene und Verwandtes*. Leipzig, 1890.

ROSE, H. J. *Primitive Culture in Greece*. London, 1925.

—— *Handbook of Greek Mythology*. 5th ed. London, 1953.

ROSTOVTZEFF, M. *A History of the Ancient World I.* 2nd ed. Oxford, 1930.

—— *The Social and Economic History of the Hellenistic World.* 2nd ed. Oxford, 1957.

—— *Social and Economic History of the Roman Empire.* Oxford, 1926.

ROUSE, W. H. D. *Greek Votive Offerings.* Cambridge, 1902.

SCHAEFFER, C. F. A. *Cuneiform Texts of Ras Shamra.* London, 1939.

SEAGER, R. B. *Excavations on the Island of Pseira, Crete.* Boston/New York, 1912.

—— *Explorations in the Island of Mochlos.* Philadelphia, 1910.

SEEBOHM, H. E. *The Structure of Greek Tribal Society.* London, 1895.

SEGRE, M. Κρητικὸς πόλεμος RF 11 (1933).

SELTMAN, C. *Greek Coins,* 2nd ed. London, 1955.

—— *Masterpieces of Greek Coinage.* Oxford, 1949.

SEMENOFF, A. *Antiquitates iuris publici Cretensium.* Petrograd, 1893.

SHREWSBURY, J. F. D. *The Plague of the Philistines.* London, 1964.

SIMON, J. *Zur Inschrift von Gortyn.* Vienna, 1886.

SINCLAIR, T. A. *Hesiod, Works and Days.* London, 1932.

SINGER, C., HOLMYARD, E. J., HALL, A. R., and WILLIAMS, T. I. (editors). *A History of Technology.* 1–2. Oxford, 1954–6.

SPRATT, T. A. B. *Travels and Researches in Crete.* London, 1865.

STUBBINGS, F. H. *Mycenaean Pottery from the Levant.* Cambridge, 1951.

SVORONOS, J. N. *Numismatique de la Crète ancienne.* Macon, 1890.

—— *Sur les* λέβητες *(espèce de monnaies) de Crète et la date de la grande inscription contenant les lois de Gortyne,* BCH 12.

SWINDLER, M. H. *Cretan elements in the Cults and Ritual of Apollo.* Bryn Mawr, 1913.

SWOBODA, H. *Lehrbuch der griechischen Staatsaltertümer.* 6th ed. Tübingen, 1913.

TARN, W. W., and GRIFFITH, G. T. *Hellenistic Civilisation.* 3rd ed. London, 1952.

TAYLOR, A. E. *The Laws of Plato.* London, 1934.

THENON, L. *Une inscription archaïque de Gortyne,* RA 8.

THIEL, J. H. *De Feminarum apud Dores condicione.* M 57.

THOMSON, G. *Aeschylus and Athens.* 2nd ed. London, 1946.

—— *Aeschylus, Oresteia.* Cambridge, 1938.

—— *Aeschylus, Prometheus Bound.* Cambridge, 1932.

—— *From Religion to Philosophy,* JHS 73.

—— *Studies in Ancient Greek Society.* 1: *The Prehistoric Aegean.* 2nd ed. London, 1954. 2: *The First Philosophers.* London, 1955.

—— *The Greek Calendar.* JHS 63.

—— *The Greek Language.* Cambridge, 1960.

—— *The Wheel and the Crown.* CR 59.

THOMSON, J. A. K. *Studies in the Odyssey.* Oxford, 1914.

THUMB, A. *Handbuch der griechischen Dialekte.* 2te Auflage von E. Kieckers. Heidelberg, 1932.

THURNWALD, R. *Economics in Primitive Communities.* London, 1932.

TOD, M. N. *Greek Inscriptions II,* GR I.

—— *International Arbitration amongst the Greeks.* Oxford, 1913.

—— *Teams of Ball-players at Sparta,* ABSA 10.

TREVOR-BATTYE, A. *Camping in Crete.* London, 1913.

TRISP, A. *Die Fragmente der griechischen Kultschriftsteller.* Geisen, 1914.

TRITSCH, F. J. *Die Agora von Elis und die altgriechische Agora. Jahresh.* 27.

—— *Die Stadtbildungen des Altertums und die griechische Polis.* K 22.

—— *Lycian, Luwian and Hittite. Symbolae Hrozny, Pt. 3. Archiv Orientální.* 18.1–2.

TYLOR, E. B. *Primitive Culture.* 3rd ed. London, 1891.

TYPALDOS, I. A. Ἑρμηνεία τῆς ἐν Γόρτυνι τῆς Κρήτης τῷ 1884 ἀνακαλυφθείσης ἐπιγραφῆς. Athens, 1887.

URE, P. N. *The Origin of Tyranny.* Cambridge, 1922.

VAN DER MIJNSBRUGGE, M. *The Cretan Koinon.* New York, 1931.

VAN DER POST, L. *The Lost World of the Kalahari.* London, 1958.

VAN EFFENTERRE, H. *À propos du serment des Drériens.* BCH 61.

—— *Inscriptions archaïques crétoises.* BCH 70.

—— *La Crète et le monde grec de Platon à Polybe.* Paris, 1948.

—— *Querelles crétoises,* REA 44.

—— *Voies et places publiques au Nord-Ouest du palais de Mallia,* BCH 87.

VAN GENNEP, A. *L'état actuel du problème totémique.* Paris, 1920.

—— *Les rites de passage.* Paris, 1909. *The Rites of Passage.* London, 1960.

VASILIEV, A. A. *History of the Byzantine Empire.* Madison, 1961.

VENTRIS, M., and CHADWICK, J. *Documents in Mycenaean Greek.* Cambridge, 1956.

—— *Evidence for Greek Dialect in the Mycenaean Archives.* JHS 73.

VOLLGRAFF, W. *Inscription d'Argos (Traité entre Knossos et Tylissos).* BCH 37.

WACE, A. J. B. *A Cretan Statuette in the Fitzwilliam Museum.* Cambridge, 1927.

—— *Chamber Tombs of Mycenae. Arc.* 82.

—— *Excavations at Mycenae.* ABSA 25.

—— *Mycenae.* Princeton, 1949.

—— *Mycenae, Ant.* 10.

—— *Mycenae 1939.* JHS 59.

—— *The Treasury of Atreus, Ant.* 14.

—— and STUBBINGS, F. H. (ed.) *A Companion to Homer.* London, 1962.

WACKERNAGEL, J. *Sprachliche Untersuchungen zu Homer, Gl.* 7.

WADE-GERY, H. T. *The Poet of the Iliad.* Cambridge, 1952.

WALBANK, F. W. *Polybius on the Roman Constitution.* CQ 37.

WALLON, H. *Histoire de l'esclavage dans l'antiquité.* 2nd ed. Paris, 1879.

WEBSTER, H. *Primitive Secret Societies.* 2nd ed. New York, 1932.

WELCKER, F. G. *Kleine schriften.* Bonn, 1844–67.

—— *Griechische Götterlehre.* Göttingen, 1857–63.

WESTERMANN, W. L. *Between Slavery and Freedom,* AHR 50.

WESTERMARCK, E. A. *Origin and Development of Moral Ideas.* London, 1906–8.

—— *The History of Human Marriage.* 5th ed. London, 1921.

WIDE, S. *Lakonische Kulte.* Leipzig, 1893.

WIDENGREN, G. *The King and the Tree of Life in Ancient Near Eastern Religion.* Uppsala Universitets Årsskrift, 1951–4.

WILAMOWITZ-MOELLENDORFF, U. VON. *Der Glaube der Hellenen.* Berlin, 1931–2.

WILLETTS, R. F. *Aristocratic Society in Ancient Crete.* London, 1955.

—— *A Neotas at Dreros?* H 85.3.

—— *Cretan Cults and Festivals.* London/New York, 1962.

—— *Cretan Eileithyia.* CQ 8.3–4.

—— *Europa,* E 1.

—— *Freedmen at Gortyna,* CQ 4 (1954).

—— Καρποδαῖσται. *Philol.* 105.1–2.

—— *Some Elements of Continuity in the Social Life of Ancient Crete.* IRSH 2.3.

—— *The Historical Importance of the Gortyn Laws,* BHJ 3.

—— *The Myth of Glaukos and the Cycle of Birth and Death.* K 37.

—— *The Neodamodeis.* CP 49.

—— *The Neotas of Gortyna,* H.82.

—— *The Servile Interregnum at Argos.* H 87.4.

—— *Cretan* καδεστάς in Proceedings of the First International Cretological Congress, *Kretika Khronika* (1961–2).

WOOLLEY, L. *A Forgotten Kingdom.* London, 1953.

WU TA-K'UN. *An Interpretation of Chinese Economic History.* PP 1.1.

WYCHERLEY, R. E. *How the Greeks Built Cities.* London, 1949.

XANTHOUDIDES, S. A. *The Vaulted Tombs of Mesara.* London, 1924.

—— *Cretan Expedition,* AJA 2 (1898).

—— Εὐνομία. REG 25.

ZERVOS, C. *L'Art de la Crète.* Paris, 1956.

ZHEBELEV, S. A. *Khersonesskaya prisyaga,* Izvestiya Akademii Nauk VII Seriya (Otdelenie obschestvennykh nauk) no. 10.

ZIEBARTH, E. *Aus dem griechischen Schulwesen.* 2nd ed. Leipzig/Berlin, 1914.

—— *Das griechische Vereinswesen,* Leipzig, 1896.

—— *Kulturbilder aus griechischen Städten.* 3rd ed. Leipzig/Berlin, 1919.

—— *Zum griechischen Schulwesen, Jahresh.* 13.

## EPIGRAPHICAL PUBLICATIONS

CIG      A. Böckh, *Corpus Inscriptionum Graecarum*. Berlin, 1827–77.

Delphinion   A. Rehm, *Das Delphinion in Milet*, in *Milet: Ergebnisse der Ausgrabungen und Untersuchungen seit dem Jahre 1899*, III, 362–406. Berlin, 1914.

DHR     R. Dareste, B. Haussoullier, T. Reinach, *Recueil des inscriptions juridiques grecques*. 1 série, Paris, 1891–5; 2 série, Paris, 1898–1904.

*Die Inschriften von Magnesia am Maeander*, ed. O. Kern. Berlin, 1900.

F. Durrbach, *Choix d'Inscriptions de Délos*. Paris, 1921.

Heikel    I. A. Heikel, *Griechische Inschriften sprachlich erklärt*. Helsingfors, 1924.

Hicks-Hill   E. L. Hicks and G. F. Hill, *A Manual of Greek Historical Inscriptions*. Oxford, 1901.

IC      *Inscriptiones Creticae opera et consilio Friderici Halbherr collectae*. 1. *Tituli Cretae mediae praeter Gortynios*. Rome, 1935. 2. *Tituli Cretae Occidentalis*. Rome, 1939. 3. *Tituli Cretae Orientalis*. Rome, 1942. 4. *Tituli Gortynii*. Rome, 1950. *Curavit Margarita Guarducci*.

IG     *Inscriptiones Graecae*. Berlin, 1873–.

IGA    H. Roehl, *Inscriptiones Graecae antiquissimae praeter Atticas in Attica repertas*. Berlin, 1882.

IGR    *Inscriptiones Graecae ad res Romanas pertinentes*. Paris, 1911–27.

IIGA    H. Roehl, *Imagines inscriptionum Graecarum antiquissimarum*. 3rd ed. Berlin, 1907.

IPE     *Inscriptiones orae septentrionalis Ponti Euxini*, ed. B. Latyshev. Petersburg, 1885–1901: $1^2 =$ vol. i, 2nd ed., 1916.

*Inscr. Cos.*   *The Inscriptions of Cos*, ed. W. R. Paton and E. L. Hicks. Oxford, 1891.

*Inscr. Perg.*   *Die Inschriften von Pergamon*, in *Altertumer von Pergamon viii*, ed. M. Fraenkel. Berlin, 1890–5.

MAMA    *Monumenta Asiae Minoris Antiqua*. Manchester/London, 1928–.

Michel    C. Michel, *Recueil d'inscriptions grecques*. Paris/Brussels, 1900–27.

OGI     *Orientis Graeci Inscriptiones Selectae*, ed. W. Dittenberger. Leipzig, 1903–5.

Roberts    E. S. Roberts, *An Introduction to Greek Epigraphy*, I. Cambridge, 1887.

BIBLIOGRAPHY

Schwyzer    E. Schwyzer, *Dialectorum Graecarum exempla epigraphica potiora* (3rd ed. of P. Cauer's *Delectus inscriptionum Graecarum propter dialectum memorabilium*). Leipzig, 1923.

SGDI    *Sammlung der griechischen Dialekt-Inschriften*, ed. H. Collitz, F. Bechtel, O. Hoffmann. Göttingen, 1884–1915.

SIG    *Sylloge Inscriptionum Graecarum*, ed. W. Dittenberger. 3rd ed. Leipzig, 1915–24.

Solmsen    F. Solmsen, *Inscriptiones Graecae ad inlustrandas dialectos selectae* (4th ed. by E. Fraenkel). Leipzig, 1930.

Tod    M. N. Tod, Greek Historical Inscriptions. I., to the end of the 5th C. B.C. 2nd ed. Oxford, 1946. II, from 403 to 323 B.C. Oxford, 1948.


PERIODICALS

ABSA    *Annual of the British School at Athens*. London, 1894–.
AHR    *American Historical Review*. New York—Lancaster, 1895–.
AJA    *American Journal of Archaeology*. v.p. 1885–.
AJP    *American Journal of Philology*. Baltimore, 1880–.
AM    *Mitteilungen des deutschen archäologischen Instituts, Athenische Abteilung*. 1876–.
*Annuario*    *Annuario della regia Scuola Archeologica di Atene*. 1914–.
*Ant.*    *Antiquity*. London, 1926–.
*Arc.*    *Archaeologia*. London, 1770–.
*Arch. f. Religionswiss.*    *Archiv für Religionswissenschaft*. Freiburg im Breisgau, 1898–.
*Archiv Orientální*.    Prague, 1929–.
BCH    *Bulletin de correspondance hellénique*. Paris, 1877–.
BHJ    *University of Birmingham Historical Journal*, 1947–.
BJS    *British Journal of Sociology*. London, 1950–.
BICS    *Bulletin of the Institute of Classical Studies*. London, 1954–.
CP    *Classical Philology*. Chicago, 1906–.
CQ    *Classical Quarterly*. London, 1907–.
CR    *Classical Review*. London, 1887–.
E    *Eirene. Studia Graeca et Latina*. Prague, 1960–.
*Epigraphica*    *Epigraphica. Rivista italiana de epigrafia*. Milan, 1938–.
*Gl.*    *Glotta*. Göttingen, 1907–.
GR    *Greece and Rome*. Oxford, 1931–.
H    *Hermes*. Berlin-Wiesbaden, 1866–.
HAS    *Harvard African Studies*. Cambridge, Mass., 1917–.

Hesperia    *Hesperia: Journal of the American School of Classical Studies at Athens.* Cambridge, Mass., 1932–.

*Hist.*    *Historia, studi storici per l'antichità classica.* Milan/Rome, 1927–.

*Indogerman. Forsch.*    *Indogermanische Forschungen.* Strassburg/Berlin, 1891–.

IRSH    *International Review of Social History.* Assen/Netherlands, 1956–.

*Jahrb.*    *Jahrbuch des (kaiserlich) deutschen archäologischen Instituts.* 1886–.

*Jahresh.*    *Jahreshefte des österreichischen archäologischen Institutes.* Vienna, 1898–.

JHS    *Journal of Hellenic Studies.* London, 1880–.

JP    *Journal of Philology.* London, 1868–1920.

K    *Klio, Beiträge zur alten Geschichte.* Leipzig, 1901–.

KK    ΚΡΗΤΙΚΑ ΧΡΟΝΙΚΑ. Heraklion, 1946–.

LQR    *Law Quarterly Review.* London, 1885–.

M    *Mnemosyne.* Leiden, 1852–.

MA    *Monumenti antichi pubblicati per cura della Reale Accademia dei Lincei.* Rome/Milan, 1890–.

*Mus. It.*    *Museo italiano di antichità classica.* Florence, 1885–90.

*Num. Chron.*    *Numismatic Chronicle.* London, 1838–.

OL    *Orientalistische Literaturzeitung.* Leipzig, 1897–.

*Philol.*    *Philologus.* 1841–.

PP    *Past and Present.* London, 1951–.

RA    *Revue Archéologique.* Paris, 1844–

REG    *Revue des études grecques.* Paris, 1888–.

RF    *Rivista di filologia e di istruzione classica.* Turin, 1873–.

*Rivista di storia antica.* Padua/Messina, 1895–1910.

RL    *Rendiconti della Reale Accademia nazionale dei Lincei.* Rome, 1873–.

RM    *Rheinisches Museum für Philologie.* Frankfurt, 1842–.

RR    *Review of Religion.* New York, 1936–.

S    *Syria.* Paris, 1919–.

VDI    Вестник Древней Истории. Moscow/Leningrad, 1947–.

*Wiener Denkschr.*    *Denkschriften der Akademie der Wissenschaften in Wien, Phil.-hist.Klasse.* 1850.

# Subject Index

# Index of Deities, Persons, Places

192